Writing Without Bullshit

Also by Josh Bernoff

The Mobile Mind Shift written with Ted Schadler and Julie Ask

Empowered written with Ted Schadler

Groundswell written with Charlene Li

Writing Without Bullshit

Boost Your Career by Saying What You Mean

JOSH BERNOFF

HARPER
BUSINESS

An Imprint of HarperCollins*Publishers*

HarperCollins books may be purchased for educational, business, or sales promotional use. For information, please email the Special Markets Department at SPsales@harpercollins.com.

Portions of this material were adapted from material previously published on the author's blog at withoutbullshit.com.

FIRST EDITION

Designed by Bonni Leon-Berman

Library of Congress Cataloging-in-Publication Data has been applied for.

ISBN: 978-0-06-247715-6

21   LSC   10 9 8 7

To Dad, who taught me to be bold, clear, and honest

Disclaimer

If you follow the advice you are about to read, it will have a powerful impact on your career.

Learning to say what you mean in a bold, direct way can boost your career. Saying it the wrong way, or at the wrong time, or to the wrong person, can also get you in trouble.

While I hope these words will help you, you alone are responsible for the consequences, positive or negative, of writing without bullshit.

Contents

Part One   Change Your Perspective

1   Transcend Bullshit   3
2   Seize Your Opportunity   18

Part Two   Change What You Write

3   Move Beyond Fear   33
4   Write Short   43
5   Front-Load Your Writing   55
6   Purge Passive Voice   61
7   Replace Jargon   68
8   Eliminate Weasel Words   76
9   Be Direct   84
10 Use Numbers Wisely   92
11 Reveal Structure   107

Part Three   Change How You Write

12 Be Paranoid Early   121
13 Think First   128
14 Plan Purposefully   135
15 Unleash Creativity   144
16 Find Flow   150
17 Collaborate Without Tears   157
18 Embrace Edits   168
19 Edit Effectively   181

Part Four   Change What You Produce

20 Understand Containers   191

21 Email Thoughtfully   194

22 Master Social Media   212

23 Promote Intelligently   228

24 Craft Actionable Reports   242

Epilogue   Change the Bullshit Culture   253

Acknowledgments   257

Notes   259

Bibliography   271

Index   273

Writing Without Bullshit

Part One

Change Your Perspective

1
Transcend Bullshit

The tide of bullshit is rising.

Your email inbox is full of irrelevant, poorly written crap. Your boss talks in jargon and clichés. The websites you read are impenetrable and incomprehensible.

Bullshit is a burden on all of us, keeping us from getting useful work done.

Technology has made it breathtakingly easy for anybody to create content and distribute it to thousands of people. Unfortunately, nobody told those creators what it takes to create good content, so we're stuck wading through a deluge of drivel.

You know this is a problem. I'm here to tell you that it's also an opportunity.

Imagine for a moment that you could write boldly, clearly, and powerfully every time you sat down at the keyboard. When your email showed up in your colleagues' inboxes, it would pop. Reports you wrote would get people to sit up and take notice. Customers would respond to your marketing copy. You'd earn a reputation as a straight talker.

Why aren't you doing this yet? I know why. I've worked with thousands of people just like you, people who work in offices and need to communicate in their jobs. Here's what's stopping them—and you—from clearing away the bullshit and writing clearly.

First, you got the wrong training. In high school and college, you learned to write verbose prose to fool teachers into believing you knew what you were talking about. Those teachers implicitly taught you that bullshitting was effective.

Then, when you started working, you found yourself immersed in more babble. From the moment you sat down and read the employee manual, you were sunk. You took your cues from the people around you, people who didn't tend to tell the plain truth when they wrote things.

Finally, you learned that avoiding risk was paramount. Clarity can be dangerous because people who read what you wrote might disagree with it.

If you're okay with being a mindless component in the vast bullshit machine that is the business world, please put this book down and walk away. You can keep writing equivocal garbage, and you'll fit in just fine.

But if you'd prefer to stand out, I can show you how. It's not that hard. In fact, it's mostly a matter of connecting with your own natural ways of communicating.

I'll show you what's motivating you to write the way you do and what's stopping you from writing more clearly. Every single bad habit you've learned is tied up with your own psychology at work. As I teach you to express yourself more powerfully, I'll clear away the motivational roadblocks that are stopping you. Once you understand that psychology, you'll be on your way to making a far more powerful impression.

I will give you the courage to say what you mean.

Then I'll give you the skills, teach you the tricks, and show you how to organize your day so you get the chance to show that courage in everything you write.

If you have good ideas and express them well in writing, you'll get credit for those ideas and their clarity. You'll also get credit for your candor and integrity. Not only is that good for your career, but it feels good, too.

The Iron Imperative

Let's agree on one principle. This principle powers everything else in this book. I call it the Iron Imperative:

Treat the reader's time as more valuable than your own.

That couldn't be simpler. And yet everything that's wrong with the way businesspeople write today stems from ignoring this principle.

A marketer creates a website to describe her company. She's on a deadline and has to get input from multiple people. Eventually she gives up and cobbles together some prose that has everybody's fingerprints on it. Is her top priority the reader's time? No, it's getting the text into the site by the deadline.

A coworker emails you and a dozen others about a problem in your department. He puts down the elements in the order that they occur to him. The subject line is "I was just thinking." He's been very efficient with his own time. Is he respecting your time, too? Nope.

An analyst assembles a report to justify the actions that a city should take. He knows there will be lots of objections, and he doesn't want to sound stupid, so he includes as many justifications as possible and couches everything in passive language that hides who's responsible for any actions he recommends. He has covered his ass in a very sophisticated way. Has he considered the reader's time? Not a chance.

These people aren't inherently selfish. They're just busy. When you're busy, you worry more about yourself and your deadlines. You create text to fill spaces and do jobs. It turns out that it's not so easy to just write clear, bold prose every time. So you do the best you can.

Unfortunately, each small step toward expediency erodes your own sense of integrity. You are no longer saying what you mean. That takes a moral toll on you even as it wastes your readers' time.

This waste is even worse than it appears because we're all reading nearly all the time now. We're continually consuming massive amounts of this indifferent prose, and we're doing so on glass screens that don't make reading easy. We're surrounded by distractions.

That's why the world seems to be so full of bullshit—because we're drowning in text that was slapped together without a focus on meaning and directness.

The Iron Imperative sounds like a good idea. But even if you accept it, how can you actually put it into practice?

Measuring Meaning

When you read something that is meaningful, you learn something. You could learn what Elon Musk thinks about artificial intelligence, how much rain is going to fall in the next 24 hours, or what database strategy makes sense for your company. Meaning makes you smarter.

When I talk about bullshit, I have something very specific in mind. It's prose that makes you go, "Huh?" Bullshit is communication that wastes the reader's time by failing to communicate clearly and accurately. While that includes outright lies, lies are not the biggest problem in business communication. The biggest problem is lack of clarity. Jargon, overuse of qualifying words like "very" and "deeply," confusing passive sentences, poorly organized thinking, and just general rambling on: that's bullshit. Those are constructions that hide meaning rather than reveal it.

Because of this definition, I can actually measure bullshit. To do this, I take any passage of text and identify the words that have no real meaning. Let's take a look at an example.

Inovalon is a healthcare technology company based in Maryland. On its website, under "Who We Are," is this description:

> Inovalon is a leading technology company that combines advanced cloud-based data analytics and data-driven intervention platforms to achieve meaningful insight and impact in clinical and quality outcomes, utilization, and financial performance across the healthcare landscape. Inovalon's unique achievement of value is delivered through the effective progression of Turning Data into Insight, and Insight into Action®. Large proprietary datasets, advanced integration technologies, sophisticated predictive analytics, data-driven intervention platforms, and deep subject matter expertise deliver a seamless, end-to-end capability that brings the benefits of big data and large-scale analytics to the point of care.

To everyone outside Inovalon (and, I suspect, many inside the company), this is pretty hard to parse. But just how bad is it? Let's highlight the words that don't have meaning for most readers. I'll use bold to highlight the qualifying words that don't have a precise meaning, such as "very" and "leading." I'll also highlight words and phrases that are basically just decoration to make the description sound more impressive, such as "utilization" and "across the healthcare landscape." As for the jargon that's bound to confuse most readers, I'll use bold italic to highlight that.

Now the passage looks like this:

> Inovalon is a **leading** technology company that combines **advanced** *cloud-based data analytics* and *data-driven intervention platforms* to achieve **meaningful** insight and impact in clinical and quality outcomes, **utilization**, and financial performance **across the healthcare landscape**. Inovalon's **unique achievement of** value is delivered through the **effective** progression of Turning Data into Insight, and Insight into Action®. **Large** *proprietary datasets,* **advanced** *integration technologies,* **sophisticated** *predictive analytics, data-driven intervention platforms,* and **deep** subject matter expertise deliver a **seamless, end-to-end capability** that brings the benefits of *big data* and *large-scale analytics* to the point of care.

While you can quibble about the specific words I've chosen to highlight, we can agree that there is just too much jargon and meaningless verbiage in this passage. How much? We measure that with the meaning ratio:

$$\text{meaning ratio} = \frac{meaningful\ words}{total\ words}$$

There are 92 words in this passage. I've marked 38 as not meaningful, which means only 54 are meaningful. The meaning ratio of this passage is 59%.

That's dreadful.

Nearly half of these words are getting in the way rather than helping.

An ideal passage, of course, would have a meaning ratio of 100%. A passage with a meaning ratio of 80% is readable. But once you get below 70%, you're in bullshit territory. This passage reads as bullshit because nearly half of it is not communicating anything useful.

I'm going to poke fun at lots of awful language in this book. But I'm actually out to solve the problem, not just laugh at it. So imagine for a moment that Inovalon has hired you to make its mission statement better. You might come up with something like this:

Inovalon has more insight into health data than anyone else. We analyze that data and apply the knowledge to help you improve care options, reduce costs, and improve compliance. We help hospitals, doctors, insurance payers, and patients. We identify gaps in care, quality, and data integrity, and apply our unique capabilities to resolving them.

We've reduced 92 words to 54. By using words like "we" and "you," Inovalon tells its customers what the company does and how it helps those customers. Ordinary humans, even health-care information professionals, can easily understand what "gaps in care, quality, and data integrity" are. We've restored the missing meaning by getting rid of the bullshit.

One Woman's Path from Powerful, Direct Communication to Success

Can writing without bullshit boost your career? Intuitively, we'd like to be the kinds of people who say what we mean when we write. But does it make a difference?

I've been lucky to interact with dozens of great communicators in my career. I'm not talking about professional writers, either. I'm talking about intelligent, hardworking folks who found that candor was their ticket to success.

For example, there's Diane Hessan. Diane got an MBA and then went to work at General Foods, where she was a product manager for Brim coffee. She took what she learned and joined a small training company called the Forum Corporation as product manager for their sales training product.

At Forum, a mentor named John Humphrey taught her how to communicate as efficiently as possible. His key principle in any discussion was simple: "Net it out in three clear points." In other words, what does the reader or listener really need to know, and let's not get mired in the details. Hessan learned that with impatient colleagues and skeptical customers, you have to get to the main point quickly. Taking this principle to heart, Hessan quickly grew the sales training product into a large, successful business.

She also got a reputation.

She told me about a team of people who were working late on a proposal for a client and asked to run the proposal by her. It wasn't quite up to snuff. Before offering her opinion, she asked, "Do you want to know what I really think?" The room burst out laughing because everyone knew they didn't have a choice. "That was a turning point," Hessan told me. She realized that a reputation for frankness was part of her success. "I can save myself and my team a lot of time and aggravation by being as direct as possible."

In 20 years at Forum, Hessan rose to the executive vice president level and became one of the top three executives in the company.

When she left in 1999, she launched Communispace (since renamed C Space), a company that helps generate insight from online communities. That service was a great idea, but it proved hard to explain to corporate clients—at least until Hessan figured out the plain language to explain it. "I just told them we did focus groups on steroids," she recalls. Marketers understood focus groups, and learned how online communities could quickly and continuously deliver insights from hundreds of people, not just a dozen. Communispace took off, eventually generating 40% growth for five years in a row and growing to 500-plus employees with over 250 prominent brands as clients.

While I've made it sound like Hessan and C Space took a path straight upward, anyone who has worked at a startup knows that's not how it goes. Hessan had to deal with challenges including an early cash crunch and a salesperson who got caught forging contracts. But she took on every challenge with direct, clear, and informal but bullshit-free communication. For example, in

2008 the company was coming off a great year, but Hessan was concerned about the future. Here's how she shared this in an email to her management team:

To: The Management Committee
From: Diane
February 1, 2008
Subject: We Are Not Succeeding Yet

Now that our final numbers are in for 2007, we should be mighty proud. We have doubled in size and in numbers of clients, beat our budgets by a long shot, and importantly, our retention rates are off the charts. Bravo!

Before you all go out and spend your big bonus checks too quickly, please start to think about two issues: a big problem and a big opportunity.

The problem: our people are exhausted. You hear them talk about the "crazy train", and I don't believe this is about their paychecks alone. What can we do to keep them fresh and motivated?

The opportunity: Our largest account is $1MM/year. What would a $5MM client look like? How could we go out and create a whale of an account with quintuple the impact?

I would like to talk about both of these issues at Monday's meeting. Our 2007 was outstanding, but I think we can all agree that some day, we want to look back on this past year and say, "Awww, remember 2007 when we thought we were big and successful? Ha!"

Have a good weekend, and on Monday, the champagne is on me.

This is informal but direct. It challenges her management team without undermining their credit for doing a good job. And it worked. Sales rose 50% in the next year and shortly thereafter, Communispace closed its first $5 million sale—because Hessan had helped them lay the groundwork for growth.

In 2011, the global ad agency Omnicom bought C Space for more than $100 million. Hessan went on to lead her next venture, the Startup Institute, a company that trains the next generation of startup workers.

Boost Your Career by Saying What You Mean

Could you succeed as Diane Hessan did? I've run across lots of people who have turned clear and powerful communication into career success.

Tom Cunniff failed to make it big with his band, and then joined an ad agency in the production department. To get the attention of the ad guys who needed to approve his work, he wrote them funny notes. They thought the notes were clever, so they sent Cunniff to school to learn to write copy. Eventually he left the agency and spent ten years writing short, punchy descriptions for the J. Peterman catalogue. Now he's the owner of a consultancy that helps companies with business-to-business marketing strategy. Writing is central to his success; as he says, "If you can't write clearly, you can't think clearly." He asks the simple questions that get to the heart of his clients' problems. As Cunniff sees it, "The problem is that writers don't want to get to the point, they want to show off. But it's all TL;DR [too long; didn't read]. We are all scattered on all of our devices."

Cunniff's writing about marketing stands out. In a recent blog post called "Ten Heretical Thoughts About Advertising," he bluntly states, "There is no such thing as an advertising audience anymore. Attention has been permanently scattered to the four winds. This will only get worse." And "The most important marketing activity today is to get the PRODUCT right. If you have it wrong, you can't fix it in advertising anymore." This kind of clarity attracts clients, which is one reason why Cunniff is successful.

Success through boldness and clarity isn't just for marketers. For example, consider Lionel Menchaca Jr., who started in technical support for Dell. The public relations department poached him because they needed a techie who could speak the language of their customers. He started writing press releases and, eventually, working with corporate public relations—the intermediaries between the press and senior managers like Michael Dell. In 2006, those managers tapped Menchaca to launch and write Dell's blog, one of the first corporate blogs on the Internet. Menchaca applied his technical knowledge, courage, and ability to tell the plain truth on the blog, and Michael Dell backed him up. Dell began to track direct revenue from Menchaca's blog posts; in one two-week period, it traced $125,000 in revenue to the blog. Menchaca kept blogging at Dell for seven years and has turned that experience into a director position at W2O, a digital agency. "I've learned that being simple and straightforward will always pay dividends," he says. "Taking that skill and applying it changed the trajectory of my career."

In the 1990s, Esther Schindler owned a computer store in Maine and was active on CompuServe. She learned to write clear sets of instructions, transitioned to a successful career writing articles and books, and became a pioneer in the field of "content marketing"—writing helpful online content to draw attention to companies and their products. Her philosophy fits today's distracted on-screen reader perfectly: "Always put the most important thing at the top, then back it up."

Writing isn't just for writers anymore. Everyone writes email. Every small business needs a web page. People write product descriptions, reports, and position papers. Every manager needs to present with slides. As Ann Handley says in her really useful book *Everybody Writes*, "We are all relying on words to carry our messages. We are all writers."

Businesses are now global and asynchronous. You may be working with a supplier in India one moment, a colleague in Dubuque the next, and a customer in his home office the moment after that. Chances are, they'll interact with you through the words you write.

I'd like you to start building the discipline of bullshit-free communication right now. I want you to unlearn the bloated, jargon-laden style you've been steeped in so far and switch to an impactful, direct, clear, and engaging way of communicating. You should adopt the successful habits of people like Diane Hessan, Tom Cunniff, Lionel Menchaca Jr., and Esther Schindler, because the more noisy our environment gets—the more crap that's out there—the more essential it is to respect the Iron Imperative. Don't waste your readers' time. Boost your career by saying what you mean.

Join Me on a Journey to Clarity, Candor, and Integrity

Here's what's coming in the rest of this book.

I'll spend the next short chapter explaining how we got into this mess. Unless you know what causes bullshit, you'll never escape its gravitational pull.

After that, I'll describe some principles you can use to write without bullshit in your work. I'll show you how to eliminate passive voice, weasel words, and jargon. I'll demonstrate how you can front-load your communication so it gets to the point quicker. I'll explain how best to use statistics, graphics, and other tricks to make your writing easier to skim. And above all, I'll show you how to write shorter. Shorter writing that respects the reader's time is central to the Iron Imperative. That's all in part 2.

To write this way, you'll need to change the way you write, edit, plan, and collaborate. So, next I'll describe some habits, principles, and techniques you can use to generate better ideas, write more fluidly, and get value from editors and collaborators. That's part 3.

Then you'll learn how to apply those principles in the most common forms of business writing: emails, social media posts, blog posts, press releases, and reports. That's part 4.

In the epilogue, I'll explain how you can change the bullshit culture in your company.

Like all writers, you are about to embark upon a voyage. Your objective is awareness of your own habits and why they exist. With that awareness and some tips on ways to do better, you can improve. The goal is not perfection; no writing is perfect, including this book. The goal is to understand what it takes to be better and to create content that stands out from the ordinary bullshit-laden writing that surrounds us all at work.

Learning to write this way will feel like learning yoga or skiing. You'll learn new ways to do things that will feel a little weird. You're going to have to unlearn some of what you learned about writing, which will slow you down at first. Not only that, once I've sensitized you to the forms of bullshit around you, you're going to hear my voice in your head every time you read something.

But very soon after, you'll begin to internalize these techniques. You'll be able to write shorter and faster. As you put this new, bold content out into the world, people will notice you. They will thank you for your clarity and directness. You will both feel and reflect integrity. And you might even get some of your work done a little quicker.

Wouldn't you rather be like that than be a bullshitter?

Please join us on the side of meaning. It's sunnier over here, and it smells a lot better.

2
Seize Your Opportunity

Bullshit in writing isn't new. As William Zinsser wrote in 1976, "We are a society strangling in unnecessary words, circular constructions, pompous frills, and meaningless jargon." In 1986, the philosopher Harry G. Frankfurt lamented that "one of the most salient features of our culture is that there is so much bullshit." And yet, somehow, it feels as if things have gotten a lot worse lately. A miasma of word pollution pervades our everyday business lives.

To better understand the situation, I conducted the WOBS Writing Survey from January through March 2016. Of the 547 respondents who said they write two or more hours per week for work, 61% said what they read is frequently unclear, and 81% agreed that poorly written material wastes their time. On a scale from 1 (completely ineffective) to 10 (completely effective), they rated the average effectiveness of the material they read as a pathetic 5.4. (Naturally, they rated the effectiveness of their own writing as a 6.9 on the same scale.)

How did it get this bad?

One simple sentence explains how we got here:

We spend all day long reading on screens, and what we read is unedited text created by poorly trained writers.

Let me pick that apart for you.

We spend all day long reading on screens. It's harder to get at the meaning when reading on a computer monitor or a tiny smartphone screen, surrounded by distractions.

What we read is unedited. There are considerably fewer editors and a lot more text; editing is becoming a lost art.

Created by poorly trained writers. High school and college writing teachers do not prepare workers for a world where readers read on screens.

In this chapter, I'll reveal each of these causes and explain what they mean to you, the business writer, as you attempt to communicate with your colleagues and customers.

We Spend All Day Long Reading on Screens

Reading on a screen is hard—especially when it's a five-inch smartphone screen. But increasingly, computer and phone screens are what we read all day. The professionals in the WOBS Writing Survey said they spent an average of 25.5 hours per week writing, and another 20.4 per week reading. That's 45.9 hours per week peering at text, most of it on a piece of glass.

According to Forrester Research, among adults who are online, seven out of ten already use smartphones. A salesforce .com study says those smartphone owners are spending 3.3 hours per day on their smartphones; 91% are reading email, and 75% are doing social networking. Forrester reports that half of them admit to using their phones in the bathroom. Is it any wonder that their attention span isn't what it used to be?

Forrester also says that if you're younger than 70 years old, you're more likely to read your media online than in print.

As Ben Horowitz, principal of the renowned venture capital firm Andreessen Horowitz, said in 2012, "Babies born today will probably never read anything in print."

What is this doing to the way we read?

To find out, I spoke with Josh Schwartz, chief data scientist at Chartbeat, an analytics company that measures second-by-second attention on the web. Using code embedded in the pages of its clients' websites, including those of most major media and news companies, Chartbeat determines if, how much, and how long we're actually reading a page. Schwartz told me that the average reader spends no more than 36 seconds on the average news story. When the company tested the comprehension of people who'd read a news story, they found that only 37% could answer a question about a detail at the end of the article, a result that's only slightly better than guessing.

The issue here is how reading on-screen impairs concentration. Naomi S. Baron, a professor at American University and the author of *Words Onscreen: The Fate of Reading in a Digital World*, conducted a cross-national study on it. Of the university students in her survey, 92% said it was easiest to concentrate when reading material in print compared to on a screen. As she explains, "Digital technologies are not designed for deep reading. When we use those technologies for the types of mental activity that print does so well"—especially reflective, analytical reading—"we generally don't manage the same level of focus."

Here's what this means to you.

Anything you write—an email, a web page, a tweet—must compete with everything else that your audience reads. Since they're almost certainly reading it on a screen—and probably a tiny smartphone screen—you can measure their attention span in tens of seconds. If you keep them interested long enough to learn a bit more, you can get your point across. If you don't, they'll just perceive what you wrote as bullshit.

That's why we all feel as if we are continually surrounded by bullshit.

But regardless of our attention spans, why is the text we read so lame?

A lot has to do with the decline of editing.

No One Edits What We Read

We're in the middle of a vicious cycle of content.

We read all day long. When we're not working at our desks, we're on our smartphones.

This creates an endless demand for things to read. Certainly, media companies and social networks like Facebook aim to fill that need. But so do your coworkers. Your managers feel free to demand that you read what they've written. Your colleagues think nothing of sending an email to dozens or hundreds of people.

Marketers want in on this party as well. Their ads, websites, apps, and marketing emails insinuate themselves into every pixel on your screen that's not already filled with content from media and colleagues.

The result is a constant blast of content. But that content is very different from what the previous generation of office workers consumed. Why? Let's examine what's different.

Think back for a moment to the world of 1980. The average consumer or businessperson at that time had no email, and there

FIGURE 1. In 1980, we read printed material, and an editor (or secretary) edited nearly everything we read.

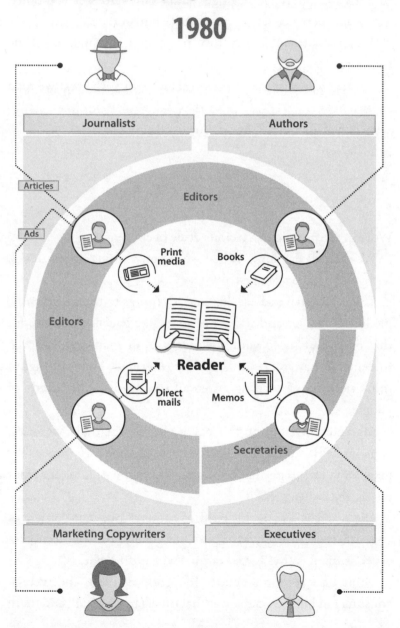

was no Internet. What we read was printed: newspapers, magazines, books, and the occasional memo.

Our reading material came from media companies that mass-produced printed material and distributed it to hundreds of thousands of magazine subscribers, book readers, and direct mail recipients. Professional writers or marketing copywriters produced it. Since it was expensive to create, it went through an experienced editor who reviewed both content and language (see figure 1). In the workplace, executives who wrote memos had secretaries to type them, and the secretaries prevented the executives from saying anything too stupid.

The picture now is vastly different. Any idiot can type and distribute content to dozens or even thousands of people, and many do, whether through email or a blog. Most of what you read comes directly from the fingertips of the person who wrote it to your eyeballs, with no editorial process (see figure 2). I don't just mean editing for grammar—no one is editing for content, either. Bullshit is communication that wastes the reader's time by failing to communicate clearly and accurately. With no editors, clarity and accuracy are hit or miss, and bullshit is inevitable.

Today's reader still reads a lot of highly edited media and ads. Even on media sites, however, that content is mingled with native ads (ads intended to look like editorial content) and contributed content (articles submitted by companies and published as content). That material doesn't get the same editorial scrutiny as regular content.

Media outlets like the *Huffington Post* don't adhere to the editorial standards of traditional media. *Forbes* has a whole slew of bloggers publishing unedited content alongside the news and

FIGURE 2. In today's read-on-screen world, we read much more, and no one edits most of what we read.

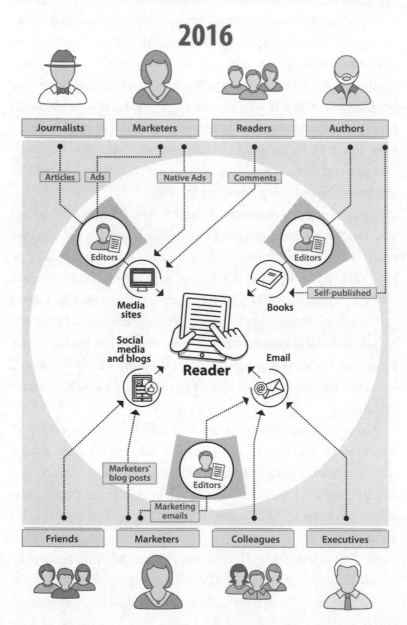

feature stories its writers create. And every article now comes complete with a set of unedited comments.

What about books? Traditional book editing is much less rigorous than it used to be (ask any author); self-published books get very little review.

Marketers must now fill a boundless set of communications channels including websites, emails, Facebook pages, Twitter feeds, and Tumblr blogs. Inexperienced writers create much of this content and often publish it with little supervision.

Inside your company, the communication model is completely different from what it once was. There are few secretaries; people communicate directly with each other, unmediated. Your inbox is filled with a random variety of first-draft emails from colleagues, managers, human resources departments, and executives.

You're a victim of the laws of supply and demand. You, I, and all the other millions of office workers consuming continuously on our various screens generate an endless demand for content. The tools available now make it possible for any random person to fill that demand. Result: an endless supply of bullshit.

We Learned to Write the Wrong Way

Writing that succeeds in the cluttered read-on-screen environment of today needs to follow a different set of rules. It needs to get quickly to the point and eschew extra verbiage, as I'll explain in detail in the rest of this book.

Is this how we learned to write in high school and college?

Unfortunately, not. We learned a completely different technique, one that's totally unsuited to reading on-screen.

Start with high school.

A high school writing teacher might have 180 students in five or six classes. The teacher's job is to prepare those students to succeed on standardized tests. That teacher was probably an English major, schooled in literary criticism.

As a student in this teacher's class, you read and critique literature. You follow a rubric called the five-paragraph essay. The first paragraph is an introduction. This is followed by three paragraphs of argumentation and a paragraph of conclusion. There are rules for what goes into each paragraph, with topic sentences and transitions. If you master this recipe, you can write a nice formulaic essay on the same topic as all the other students, and this uniformity is the only thing that makes it possible for that teacher to grade all those papers. Once you get good at following the formula, you can write the same kind of essays on standardized tests or College Board exams, and these essays then get the same cursory level of attention. If you write long and use big words, you'll probably do better. But this training won't teach you to think very deeply or make your point in a way that sticks. As one prep school teacher, Kimberly Wesley, noted, the most salient characteristic of the five-paragraph essay is "its tendency to stunt students' critical thinking abilities."

By the time your essay-writing ability has gotten you into college, you've internalized a few lessons. One is that a longer paper will probably get a better grade. You read academic writing, which is full of passive voice and jargon, and learn to imitate it to sound smart. In a survey of Stanford undergraduates, 86% admitted that they used complicated language in papers to sound more sophisticated.

If you're lucky, soon after you graduate you get a job. The first thing they do is show you the employee manual, which is full of legalese and jargon. Your colleagues are writing long cover-your-ass bullshit in the reports and emails you read. So you take those skills you learned in school and become part of the corporate bullshit machine.

We write the way we do because the educational system *trained* us to do so. But it has failed us. In the WOBS Writing Survey, only 38% of writing professionals said that their high school and college writing teachers had prepared them well for writing at work.

I can't change the way we teach writing. But if I could, here's what I would do.

I would reduce class sizes and increase the number of assignments so that students could write and get feedback frequently. Those students would rewrite their work and learn the principles of writing without bullshit.

Grading on the assignments would reward brevity, clarity, and pointed argumentation. That's right: a shorter, simpler paper would get a better grade than a long, puffed-up paper with lots of "therefores" and "howevers."

Students would practice writing emails and blog posts and research reports, not just essays, to prepare them for the real world they're about to enter.

I know this would work. I've mentored people right out of college as well as more experienced workers, intelligent people whose response to intelligent editing was to strive to create short, punchy, powerful pieces of work. These writers experienced vertigo for a short while as I undermined every assumption they had about writing . . . and then they became powerful communicators with a new sense of purpose.

I've also taught this way with high school–age homeschool students. Homeschoolers, free of the assumptions embedded in the educational system, soak up these concepts naturally. I've watched these students go on to become better writers, starting with college application essays that don't look like everybody else's. They have no idea what the five-paragraph essay is because they're writers, not assembly-line workers.

Until every writing teacher, administrator, and legislator in America reads and internalizes these messages, we're not going to change things. But that's okay. I'll settle for changing you. Just recognize that what you learned in high school and college is not what you need now to write without bullshit.

Your Opportunity

Perhaps the inevitability of a bullshit-soaked world depresses you. After all, the technological, corporate, and educational trends that brought us to a world of bullshit writing won't change anytime soon.

The trick is to see it as an opportunity.

If you write the same way as everyone else, it's hard to get ahead. And if you think you can get ahead by being a bullshitter, you'll have plenty of competition. There is always someone who is a better bullshitter than you. Once you start down that path, you'll just sink deeper and deeper.

You could take a different path. Like the homeschoolers I taught and the writers I have mentored, you could learn to clear away the crap, regain your integrity, and *say what you mean*. You could learn to uphold the Iron Imperative and treat the reader's time as more valuable than your own. Your readers will notice. And against a gray background of unmitigated bullshit, your bold writing will stand out.

What you need is courage and a clear set of instructions. I'll give you both.

Part Two

Change What You Write

3

Move Beyond Fear

I'm about to share my best practical writing advice. But I'm painfully aware that I'm following in the footsteps of distinguished writers on writing, from William Strunk Jr. and E. B. White to Steven Pinker. Maybe you've read what they wrote. But chances are you're still a long way from writing every email, report, and tweet in line with their advice. Here's why.

To begin with, they were talking to general writers. I'm talking to business writers. General writers write for a lot of reasons: to entertain, to inform, or to persuade. Business writers write for one reason: to get things done. My advice will not get you published in *The New Yorker*. It could save your job or boost your career, though.

Practical writing may sound more straightforward, but in reality, it's not, because of the fear factor. In business, fear generates bad writing habits. Feeling fear in the workplace is normal; there are risks in everything you write. You fear taking a stand, being held responsible, being wrong.

Each of us would prefer to write with integrity rather than out of fear. We want to get a reputation for telling the truth, not hiding it. But while integrity is in our hearts, fear poisons what we write. Fear destroys clarity and muddies up our writing. You cannot change how you write until you acknowledge it.

Writing advice is like health advice. I'm like the doctor telling you to eat right and exercise. You know the advice is right, but you don't follow it. Until you understand the psychology behind eating and exercise, you'll never change. Similarly, for you to accept the advice in this book, you must understand the psychology of writing at work—including the role that fear plays in your writing.

The trick is to write boldly even though you are afraid.

Understanding Fear: A Practical Example

Imagine that you're the service manager for a company that installs and services machinery at customers' locations. A machine has malfunctioned, and the customer is furious. Here's the kind of email most people would send in this situation:

From: Ted Jones, service manager
To: Sales and Service Management Committee
Subject: Analysis of service situation

As you know, I make a monthly review of the state of our service. I'll refer you to past reviews that have always shown excellent results. Our service personnel are generally considered the highest-rated regional team across the company.

In my detailed analysis of service for the last quarter, I found that things remained generally quite good. Unfortunately, among the positive results, there is one negative. One machine was unrepaired, and the customer went ahead and used it anyway. Regrettably, considerable damage was caused at the customer's site. If you are wondering who the customer was, it's Randco. We did everything possible to retain the customer, but retention may not be possible. I am hopeful that this will not end up causing legal issues, but there is the possibility of getting sued for the damage.

Please keep in mind our excellent service reputation with the other customers. I hope to be able to maintain those relationships. A review has also been undertaken to determine the cause of this issue, and to prevent a repeat of the problem.

I appreciate your attention in this matter and wish you a good end of quarter.

Ted is not fooling anybody. At this point, the recipients of this message are steaming mad because they had to work so hard to figure out what is actually happening. If you plant daisies around a pile of poo, it still stinks. Why not just point out the poo so we know not to step in it?

Because of fear, Ted wrote in a way that makes himself feel better but that actually makes his readers cringe. His problems include:

- **The noncommittal subject line.** "Analysis of service situation" doesn't clue the reader in to bad news or even indicate that this is an important email. Ted is leaving that for later.
- **The slow but ominous warm-up.** The whole first paragraph immediately tips us off to the fact that something bad is coming. The blood pressure of impatient readers starts rising right here.
- **The head fake.** "I found things remained generally quite

good" is a nonstatement. Words like "generally" don't measure anything, but they tell the reader that something bad is about to come next. As soon as the reader reads the next word, "unfortunately," any remaining goodwill instantly evaporates.

- **The passive evasions.** Passive phrases like "damage was caused" and "a review has also been undertaken" hide responsibility. Words like "retention may not be possible" and "possibility of getting sued," while not grammatically passive, similarly hide who's going to act. Writing passively insulates you from the action you describe but leaves the reader wondering who to blame.

- **The weasel words.** Meaningless intensifiers like "generally," "considerable," and "excellent" don't actually mean anything unless they're connected to some sort of statistic. They're filler. Business communication has to come straight to the point; extra words get in the way.

- **The "friendly" closing.** Ted still is so afraid of ending on a bad note that he has to include, basically, "have a nice day." It could be worse—at least he didn't use an emoticon. Face it: Cheery closings make you, the writer, feel better, but they do nothing for the readers, especially after they're done reading about a big problem like this.

Bad writing—especially writing driven by fear—creates a feeling of unease. As counterintuitive as it might seem, Ted would be better off telling the truth, boldly and with integrity. This starts with the subject line, which should immediately tell the recipients that there's a problem, and continues with statements that indicate who is responsible and what they're going to do. Here's what Ted should have written:

From: Ted Jones, service manager

To: Sales and Service Management Committee

Subject: Randco service problem and consequences

There is a problem with Randco, one of our biggest customers. On a service call, one of our techs failed to repair one of their machines. The customer was unaware of the problem and used the machine, causing several hundred thousand dollars' worth of damage.

We have taken the following actions:

- Dispatched a senior salesperson to attempt to retain Randco as a client.
- Alerted Legal to the possibility of a lawsuit for the damage.
- Reviewed the tech's service record, which was spotless except for this problem. As a result, I issued a warning but did not discipline the tech further.
- Reviewed our processes. Based on that review, I concluded that this is not part of a pattern. Our current processes will prevent it from recurring. This is consistent with our 98% quality rating in past quarters.

If you interact with Randco, be aware of the incident. Sales staff can continue to be confident about our overall service quality. If you have any further questions, please let me know.

Now Ted has put the problem at the top. He's taken responsibility for actions to remedy or mitigate the problem. He's used bullets to make it easy to scan. And the positive news intended to make people feel better is at the end, where it actually does some good, including an actual metric (98% quality) to put this in context. In the closing, Ted has told people that he's available for follow-ups.

In this new version, Ted has the courage to say what he means. He has demonstrated his integrity. By being direct, he respects the reader's time. That makes a better impression than being defensive.

Writing Boldly When You Are Afraid

Leaders write clearly and directly even when they are afraid. Take Lionel Menchaca Jr., the Dell staffer whom you met in the last chapter. One of Menchaca's first tasks as a blogger for Dell was to write a post about a battery problem that was causing Dell computers to catch fire. It would have been easy to hedge. But instead, he wrote this:

Flaming Notebook

Beyond what you've seen in the blogosphere, there is no update on the now infamous "flaming notebook" from Osaka [these four words link to a post on another blog with a picture of a Dell computer on fire]. We replaced the customer's computer and are still investigating the cause. We think it was a fault in a lithium ion battery cell.

Dell's engineering teams are working with the Consumer Product Safety Commission and a third-party failure analysis lab to determine the root cause of this failure and to ensure we take all appropriate measures to help prevent a recurrence. By the way, lithium ion batteries are used in billions of notebooks, mp3 players, PDAs and cell phones these days.

Menchaca was pretty nervous about this post, but told the truth as he knew it. Dell founder and CEO Michael Dell backed him up, which is what enabled Menchaca to go on to become Dell's primary blogger and a respected member of Dell's social media team. With this blog post as a foundation, Dell continued to communicate with its customers, ultimately agreeing to replace over 4 million batteries.

Here's another example: John W. Henry was publisher of the *Boston Globe* when the paper switched delivery companies, resulting in thousands of undelivered papers and furious customers. Rather than make excuses, he wrote this at the top of the editorial page:

We apologize to our loyal readers
The Globe's responsibility to this community is to bring it the news. I would like to share some news now about why we have failed to meet this objective for many readers over the past 10 days, how we are working to fix the problems, and a bit about the root causes.

First, I want to personally apologize to every Boston Globe subscriber who has been inconvenienced. We recognize that you depend on us, and that we've let you down. We're working around the clock on a variety of fronts to solve this. To that end, I also want to thank everyone at the Globe who pitched in to get some 20,000 Sunday papers delivered last weekend. [The article goes on to describe in some detail what went wrong and how the *Globe* is fixing it.]

I can only hope that your own writing will not deal primarily with disasters like unrepaired and dangerous equipment, products that burst into flames, and companies that can't get their primary product into customers' driveways. But even in more mundane situations, fear lurks at the back of every worker's mind. When you understand the fear, you can move beyond it to write with integrity—to say what you mean.

For Women Especially, Bold Writing Can Make a Difference

When I wrote the first draft of this book, my editor suggested that I address differences in how this advice might apply to women. "Why should it make a difference?" I thought. But then I reached out to the women who read my blog and found that the topic touched a nerve.

In person-to-person interactions in the workplace, gender matters. Women told me that if they were bold, they risked being seen as shrill or bitchy. "Women use qualifiers because when we don't, men perceive us as being hostile," said one. "I sit in many meetings each year and watch men speak over women, get the floor more readily, project more forceful opinions. I hear women apologize and cede valid points when neither is necessary," said another.

Deborah Tannen explores these perceptions in her book *Talking from 9 to 5*. As she explains, "it is common to hear that a particular woman lacks confidence or a particular man is arrogant. While we think of these as individual weaknesses, under-confidence and arrogance are disproportionately observed in women and men respectively, because they result from an over-abundance of ways of speaking that are expected of males and females." That is, women are supposed to defer, and men are supposed to speak up.

Clearly, there's a problem here. When girls are young, parents and teachers tend to reward more deferential behavior, even as they encourage and tolerate boys who speak up and interrupt. It's common for women, especially those just starting out in the working world, to apologize or soften what they say in situations where a man might challenge those around him. There are far fewer bold women than men at work.

So it's not just fear that a woman expressing herself must deal with. It is the societal pressure to smooth things over and get along with people. Women unfairly get the responsibility of making sure that everything and everybody is doing just fine. In person, this leads to apologies, hedged statements, and valid opinions that don't get stated.

I can't fix the way men and women speak to one another at work. But I can fix the way they write. And in writing, a woman can reduce this disadvantage.

You can think carefully about what you write, especially in email, and make it as direct and factual as possible.

If you have a tendency to apologize, qualify, or use weasel words, you can edit those out before sending what you have written.

Amber Naslund, an author who is also the senior vice president of marketing of the technology company Sysomos, has found that both writing and speaking directly have benefited her career. As she explains, "I think I lost some of the fear of speaking and writing directly when I realized that being criticized or even disliked was a far smaller consequence than being invisible." Writing can impress; 65% of the women in the WOBS Writing Survey agreed that they made a strong, positive impression on others with their writing. (For men, the number was only slightly higher: 70%.)

While some people perceive writing authored by a woman differently from how they'd perceive the same writing authored by a man, the biases are weaker in written material, and more easily overcome. Men won't perceive a woman who is bold and clear in writing as shrill. When writing, far more than when speaking, good ideas expressed well will get writers the credit they deserve, regardless of their gender or personality. If you want to boost your career and be more visible, learn to say what you mean in writing.

The Tools to Be Bold

In the next few chapters, I will teach you to write shorter, despite your instincts to include extra words to cover your ass. I will teach you to put your conclusion up front, instead of slowly leading up to it. I'll show you how to be clear, rather than to hedge with passive voice, jargon, and weasel words. In each chapter, you'll learn not only why it makes sense to write the way I've described but also what's been stopping you from doing so.

I'll start in the next chapter with the most important thing you can do to communicate better: write shorter.

4

Write Short

Use fewer words.

Of all the ways to communicate boldly and powerfully in a noisy world, this is the most effective. Get to the point quickly, deliver your message, and let readers get on with the rest of their day. Remember the Iron Imperative:

Treat the reader's time as more valuable than your own.

In the WOBS Writing Survey, we asked business writers what problems frequently made the material they read less effective (see figure 3). They cited one problem more than any other: 65% agreed that the material they read was frequently too long. (And 45% admitted that what they *wrote* was often too long, as well.)

Why are you still wasting people's time with writing that is too long? Insecurity. You're afraid to get right to the point; you need to warm up. You say the same thing several different ways since you're not sure which is best. It takes you a while to figure out what you're saying. You add words to hedge.

Your ideal should be tight writing. Eliminate everything you don't need. The tighter you write, the more persuasive you will be. As Roy Peter Clark says in his masterful book *How to Write Short: Word Craft for Fast Times,* "During revision, I realize that

FIGURE 3. Most frequent problems with material professionals read or write.

In the material you read/write, which of the problems listed here occur frequently enough to make the material significantly less effective?

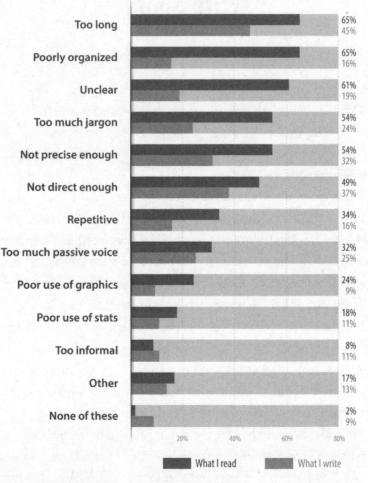

Source: WOBS Writing Survey, January–March 2016.
Base: 547 business professionals who write in English two or more hours per week, excluding email.

90 percent of my cuts are helpful." Don't just trim the fat. Lop off the stuff you liked but that isn't helping enough.

Tom Cunniff, the marketing consultant we met in chapter 1, suggests, "When you write anything, remove the first sentence. If it still makes sense, remove the second sentence. Stop only if you've lost the meaning. Almost everything I write, even a Facebook post, I ask: can it be shorter, can it be simpler, can it be crisper?"

While an editor can help you with this, you must learn to do it yourself. You won't have an editor to read every blog post, tweet, or email you send. Learn the habit of writing short.

How? I've organized a few tricks for you, listed in the order you should use them, starting with broad advice and going down to the line-editing level:

- **Edit everything.** Make it a habit. No one writes tight prose on the first draft. You need time and effort to get the words out of your head and onto the page. Admit your imperfection. Write, and allow time to self-edit. With practice, your drafts will get tighter, but you'll always need to edit.
- **Aim for a word count.** Your emails should be under 250 words. Your blog posts should be under 750. Learn the feel of a 100-, 300-, 500-, or 1,000-word hunk of prose. Imagine that words cost $10 each. How much can you afford to spend, and where can you economize? A word count makes brevity a concrete goal.
- **Say what you really mean.** Sometimes you have to draft a whole piece to understand what you really mean. That's okay, as long as you go back and get rid of the parts that no longer apply. Get rid of text that doesn't support your main point.

- **Start boldly.** Introductory text is wasteful—scrap it. Your first 50 words should intrigue the reader. Start with a bold statement, not a hedge or an apology: "We need to rethink the way we do customer service," or "Are we ready to expand geographically?" If you must write some introductory text to get warmed up, delete it on the next editing pass. You'll find you can live without it. (There's more on how to front-load your writing in the next chapter.)

- **Organize relentlessly.** In the WOBS Writing Survey, 65% of business writers said the material they read is frequently poorly organized, and 34% complained it was repetitive. Disorganized, repetitive content is wasteful. Have you hit the same point in several paragraphs or sections? Pull them together and eliminate the redundancy. Reorganize prose around the main points; pull the material that supports those points together in one place. The result is not just shorter; it's easier for readers to comprehend.

- **Prune sections and arguments.** If you've got five sections, could you make do with three or four? Could you cut a whole paragraph without weakening the argument? Have you given four examples when two would suffice? The point is not to show how much you know; it is to *save the reader time.* Removing weak or redundant material makes your whole piece stronger. Cut. Cut more. If you can't stand it, get someone else to edit and tell you which parts are weakest. Remember, adding words to a weak argument makes it weaker. Getting rid of it altogether may be an improvement.

- **Use bullets or tables.** Lists written out in prose (e.g., "Firstly," "Secondly," or "On the one hand," "Alternatively") take up extra space. Where possible, convert to a bulleted list. Bold the first phrase or sentence to make things easier to parse. For information that's sufficiently structured, tables pack a lot of information into an easily understood package. (See chapter 11 for more suggestions on efficient ways to add structure to your writing.)

- **Use graphics.** A simple diagram is often easier to comprehend than a lump of prose. It allows you to make a statement and support it without having to go into extraneous detail. But keep the graphic simple; don't just replace tangled prose with impenetrable pictures.
- **Trim connective tissue.** All the "therefores" and "now, let's continue withs" take up space, both on the screen and in the reader's brain. Look for long sentences and break them into shorter ones. This makes prose easier to digest. Transitions between sections need be only one sentence, such as "Now that we've addressed pricing, let's examine distribution."
- **Delete weasel words and qualifiers.** Every "very," "considerable," or "on the other hand" not only weakens your prose, it makes it longer. Review what you've written and get rid of qualifying words. Make specific true statements rather than broad generalizations with qualifiers. (For more detail on this, see chapter 8.)

Important Writing Should Be Short

Let's look at a famous example. Microsoft acquired mobile phone maker Nokia in April 2014. Stephen Elop, who was CEO of Nokia, continued to manage his part of the company as a division under Microsoft. About three months after the acquisition, he sent an impenetrable 1,100-word missive, intended to explain the changes at the division, to all Nokia employees. Here's most of it (to be merciful, I've removed some pieces, but the full version is on the web if you want to see it):

Hello there,

Microsoft's strategy is focused on productivity and our desire to help people "do more." As the Microsoft Devices Group, our role is to light up this strategy for people. We are the team creating the hardware that showcases the finest of Microsoft's digital work and digital life experiences, and we will be the confluence of the best of Microsoft's applications, operating systems and cloud services.

To align with Microsoft's strategy, we plan to focus our efforts. Given the wide range of device experiences, we must concentrate on the areas where we can add the most value. The roots of this company and our future are in productivity and helping people get things done. Our fundamental focus—for phones, Surface, for meetings with devices like PPI, Xbox hardware and new areas of innovation—is to build on that strength. While our direction in the majority of our teams is largely unchanging, we have had an opportunity to plan carefully about the alignment of phones within Microsoft as the transferring Nokia team continues with its integration process.

It is particularly important to recognize that the role of phones within Microsoft is different than it was within Nokia. Whereas the hardware business of phones within Nokia was an end unto itself, within Microsoft all our devices are intended to embody the finest of Microsoft's digital work and digital life experiences, while accruing value to Microsoft's overall strategy. Our device strategy must reflect Microsoft's strategy and must be accomplished within an appropriate financial envelope. Therefore, we plan to make some changes.

We will be particularly focused on making the market for Windows Phone. In the near term, we plan to drive Windows Phone volume by targeting the more affordable smartphone segments, which are the fastest growing segments of the market, with Lumia. In addition to the portfolio already planned . . . [*Five and a half paragraphs, 464 words, about products and locations omitted.*]

In short, we will focus on driving Lumia volume in the areas where we are already successful today in order to make the market for Windows Phone. With more speed, we will build on our success in the affordable smartphone space with new products offering more differentiation. We'll focus on acquiring new customers in the markets where Microsoft's services and products are most concentrated. And, we'll continue building momentum around applications.

We plan that this would result in an estimated reduction of 12,500 factory direct and professional employees over the next year. These decisions are difficult for the team, and we plan to support departing team members with severance benefits.

More broadly across the Devices team, we will continue our efforts to bring iconic tablets to market in ways that complement our OEM partners, power the next generation of meetings & collaboration devices and thoughtfully expand Windows with new interaction models. With a set of changes already implemented earlier this year in these teams, this means there will be limited change for the Surface, Xbox hardware, PPI/meetings or next generation teams.

We recognize these planned changes are broad and have very difficult implications for many of our team members. We will work to provide as much clarity and information as possible. Today and over the coming weeks leaders across the organization will hold town halls, host information sharing sessions and provide more details on the intranet.

The team transferring from Nokia and the teams that have been part of Microsoft have each experienced a number of remarkable changes these last few years. We operate in a competitive industry that moves rapidly, and change is necessary. As difficult as some of our changes are today, this direction deliberately aligns our work with the cross company efforts that Satya [Microsoft CEO Satya Nadella] has described in his recent emails. Collectively, the clarity, focus and alignment across the company, and the opportunity to deliver the results of that work into the hands of people, will allow us to increase our success in the future.

Regards,

Stephen

How would you feel if you worked for Nokia and received this? It's incomprehensible. Even worse, about 80% of the way through there's a little note about 12,500 people losing their jobs, which has to be close to a world record for burying the lede. (The "in short" halfway through is particularly galling.) Elop's main message, inadvertent though it may be, is "I'm head of your division, and I'm full of bullshit."

If you were Stephen Elop (or someone advising him), how would you fix this?

Let's start with the target word count, which ought to be about 250 words for an email this important. Keep it short. You'll be sure everybody reads it, *and* you'll make sure you focus on the most important messages.

In the "Say what you really mean" department, these are the main messages of this missive:

- We're laying off 12,500 people, and we have a plan to communicate that.
- Our focus is on devices that support Microsoft's software goals.
- We're changing the management structure.
- We're changing where we do engineering.

So our rewrite will focus on these four issues. We can cut whole paragraphs that don't support the main message. We can combine the stuff about the layoffs and the places where Microsoft does engineering. And for what remains, we can do some surgery, deleting redundant text and passive voice for a clearer, more direct message.

Here's a far better email:

Subject: Significant changes in the Microsoft Devices Group
As I'm sure you expected, our organization must change to be an effective part of Microsoft. In this email, I'll describe our goals, our future staffing levels, and our new management structure.

The driver behind these changes is our new role within Microsoft. While Nokia focused on selling hardware, now we must focus on adding value to Microsoft software and experiences, including Windows Phone software on our Lumia devices.

We need to be more efficient. We will put Jo Harlow over a single phone business unit. We will concentrate our phone engineering efforts in Salo, Finland (for future high-end Lumia products), and Tampere, Finland (for more affordable devices). We will ramp down engineering work in Oulu, Beijing, and San Diego. We will continue application software development in Espoo and Lund. [*This short paragraph summarizes the five paragraphs I omitted from the original.*]

Combining these engineering reductions with cuts in manufacturing, we will cut 12,500 factory direct and professional employees over the next year.

Today and over the coming weeks, leaders across the organization will hold town halls, host information-sharing sessions, and provide more details on the intranet. They will be informing those whose positions have been cut and explaining severance benefits.

As difficult as some of our changes are today, this direction aligns our work with the cross company efforts that our CEO, Satya Nadella, has described in his recent emails. I expect to explain these directions further as the company moves forward.

Regards,

Stephen

That's 240 words. Yes, it leaves many questions unanswered, but Elop's rambling original message didn't answer those questions, either. It's far better to cover the subject matter clearly and

FIGURE 4. Tips for writing shorter.

Tip	What to do	Why it helps	Why it's hard
Edit everything.	Always self-edit what you write.	After the draft is done, keep only the best bits.	You don't set aside editing time.
Aim for a word count.	Determine target count at the start.	It makes your brevity goal concrete.	Hard limits cramp your style.
Say what you really mean.	After drafting, figure out your true meaning.	You can rewrite to make that meaning clear.	You must cut cherished stuff that's off topic.
Start boldly.	Get rid of introductory warm-up text.	It's more powerful to get right to the point.	It's uncomfortable to open with no intro.
Organize relentlessly.	Combine related points; cut redundancy.	Result is shorter and easier to comprehend.	Reorganizing and rewriting is hard work.
Prune sections and arguments.	Delete extra arguments and examples.	Three strong points beat five weak ones.	You want to show off how much you know.
Use bullets or tables.	Replace prose with lists or tables.	Lists make structure visually explicit.	It forces you to think in rigid structures.
Use graphics.	Replace text with simple diagrams.	Pictures are easier to comprehend.	You're a writer, not an illustrator.
Trim connective tissue.	Reduce linking words and transition text.	Connecting words make noisy prose.	You like to show when you're shifting gears.
Delete weasel words and qualifiers.	Get rid of qualifiers like "very" and "generally."	Qualifiers make writing mushy.	You're worried you might be wrong.

leave the rest for a follow-up. I've cut the warm-up paragraphs, focused on the actual message, written in a clear and direct way, and indicated what will come next. As difficult as a change like this is (and at Nokia, it was incredibly difficult), a tight message communicates that you know what you're doing and will follow up in an appropriate way.

Figure 4 summarizes strategies to keep writing short and tight.

5
Front-Load Your Writing

Get to the point.

The reader's attention is limited. You must drive home your point in the first few words. Interest your reader, and you can explain further. Fail that interest, and you won't get the chance.

Different writing formats offer different tools. Emails have subject lines. Documents and blog posts have titles. Reports have executive summaries. And all forms of writing have opening sentences, or as journalists call them, ledes. But regardless of format, the objective is the same: deliver the main idea, up front, in as few words as possible.

Barbara Minto's book *The Pyramid Principle* has been influencing business thinkers for decades. As she explains, "Controlling the sequence in which you present your ideas is the single most important act necessary to clear writing. The clearest sequence is always to give the summarizing idea before you give the individual ideas being summarized." As the world has gotten noisier, this concept has become even more important.

Seasoned writers have internalized this principle in the way they write for people who read on a screen. Esther Schindler, who has written hundreds of magazine articles and content marketing pieces, puts it this way: "When you have the urge to write a whole long story, write the summary sentence instead. Write the one thing you want someone to know after reading this, and then back it up. If people know where you're heading, they're more willing to read it."

I call this "front-loading" your writing: putting the conclusion up front.

To master this way of thinking, you must invert what you learned in school about reasoning and writing. You learned to start with a warm-up, then reason deductively, starting from first principles and reaching a conclusion. Business readers have no time for warm-ups and lack the patience for extended reasoning unless they know the payoff up front. So start with bold statements and conclusions. Then follow with the reasoning that got you there. That way, readers who don't read the whole document will still benefit from reading your conclusion. (Until you get used to writing this way, you'll have to write longer pieces, delete the warm-ups, and insert the conclusions up front. Do this a few times and you'll learn the habit of front-loading things to save writing time.)

Let's look at how front-loading applies in three forms of business writing: emails, documents or blog posts, and short text messages.

Emails: Front-Load Subject Lines and Opening Sentences

The objective of an email, whether to a colleague or a prospect, is to communicate an idea. If the recipient gets intrigued enough to open it—and if the content matches the promise in the subject line—then you've succeeded. Otherwise, you've failed.

Your subject line is crucial. Focus on accuracy and brevity. Ask yourself, If all they read is the subject line, will I still have communicated something useful? Here are some good examples for emails to colleagues:

July sales exceed quotas by 20%
We must respond quickly to competitor's new features
Change in benefits requires your attention

Here are some terrible subject lines:

Some things that are on my mind right now
Three ideas about our product
Time to get ready for a big change

The first three subject lines promise content. The second three could be anything; recipients might open them but might not. Remember, too, that as people reply or forward the email, the subject line becomes a heading for the discussion. Modern email systems like Gmail organize the email into threads based on the topic. What's in that thread called "Some things that are on my mind right now"? Pretty tough to know.

If an email is at all important, take 30 seconds to rewrite the subject line after you've written the body of the email.

Don't disappoint readers once they open the email. Tell them your objective and the action you want in the opening sentences. For example, "Our biggest competitor just created a feature that allows customers to order from mobile in one tap. This is going to be popular, so we need a response soon." Get right to the point. There is no time for a leisurely narrative ("I was reading our competitor's website, and I noticed that . . .").

Having announced your main idea, use the rest of the email to justify it. That shouldn't be more than 250 words.

If the email is to a customer or prospect rather than a colleague, the same principles apply with slight differences. While business emails get the benefit of the doubt, readers assume marketing emails will be worthless, which is why marketers have specialized in techniques that charm you into opening an email. Stating a problem is one of the most honest. It gets the right people to open the email: people who have that problem. An email with the subject "Are your rugs getting musty again?" will reach the right people for a carpet cleaner. Tell the customer how you'll solve the problem in the opening sentences.

For more detail on emails that work, see chapter 21.

Documents: Hook People with the Title and Opening

If you expect to distribute a significant document like a report to a bunch of people, the title has a big job to do. It has to be interesting enough to make the document seem worth reading. And it must create a way to talk about the document. For example, the internal analysis paper that the *New York Times* created to address digital strategy was simply called "Innovation." This is a terrible title. "Saving journalism in the digital era" would have been more compelling and descriptive. Larger documents can also use subtitles to elaborate on content.

A document of more than ten pages also needs an executive

summary. Again, put your intuition aside and *don't summarize in the summary*. Think of it more as a movie trailer, which includes the bits of the movie most likely to make you want to go see it. A great executive summary is filled with proper names and numbers that intrigue. Chapter 24 has more tips on writing titles and summaries for reports.

Here's a counterintuitive thought: the filename for your document *also* carries information. "Buick sales analysis Q4 16" is easy to spot and sort with other quarterly sales reports. "Sales Report v6" is not. Don't waste readers' time with generic filenames.

Blog Posts: Write Titles That Intrigue Both People and Google

A blog post is like a cross between a document and an email. Its title must fascinate readers and allow them to reference it easily.

When it comes to titles, you must also consider search engine optimization (SEO). SEO is the science of including words in online content for the purpose of ranking higher in searches on Google and other sites. And while search is important, it's not as important as clarity. Stuffing too many search words into titles makes them hard to parse. A clear, fascinating title works great, not just at the top of a post but in the snippet of text that entices people to click on a Google search result or an embedded link on Facebook.

Like emails, blog posts need to get to the point in a few sentences. Avoid lame-ass warm-ups—just delete them and start with something meaty. Remember, those first few sentences also appear in blog subscribers' emails and in Google search results, so make them meaningful. For more detail on effective blog posts, see chapter 20.

You can extend these ideas to other forms, such as book titles or press releases. But regardless of the form of communication, remember to balance clarity, brevity, fascination, and descriptiveness in your titles and summaries. They're the most important part of your document; reconsider and rewrite them before you publish or hit Send.

6

Purge Passive Voice

Passive voice makes your writing muddy. It has its uses, but you're using it far too often. Everyone does.

Passive voice interferes with direct and powerful writing. I will sensitize you to your passive habit and then show you how to fix it.

First off, what is passive voice?

In a passive voice sentence, the subject of the sentence is not the actor performing the action. The sentence starts instead with the noun that the action is done *to*. The missing actor at the start of the sentence obscures the meaning. For example, in the sentence "Attention must be paid to the state of our nation," who is supposed to pay attention? That's the missing actor. Grammatically, passive voice sentences include some form of the verb "to be" ("is," "was," "ought to be," "have been," "should be," or "can be," for example) plus a past participle. Often, it's easier to just use the zombies test: if you can add "by zombies" after the verb and it still makes grammatical sense, it's passive voice. ("Attention must be paid by zombies . . .")

Every passive voice sentence sets up uneasiness in readers' minds. They wonder what unseen force is responsible for the actions they're reading about, because the passive hides the "who" in sentences. The more passive voice, the more uneasy people get. This uneasiness wastes readers' time, and that violates the Iron Imperative.

Fixing the passive will force you to think about who is acting in the sentences you write. This is a discipline that you should adopt because it improves meaning as well as readability. Bold writers don't hide behind passive constructions.

I've cured many writers of the passive habit. I can cure you, too. All it takes are the five Rs: recognize, raise awareness, reconsider, rewrite, and retrain.

Think of this process the way you'd think of changing your diet. Let's say you want to cut down on sugar. First you need to recognize why sugar is a problem. Then you need to raise your awareness of all the places sugar lurks in your diet. You must reconsider your sugar habit. Then you'll need to replace the sugary foods with stuff that's better for you. Finally, you need to retrain yourself with better habits to make the change permanent.

With passive voice, as with sugar, your objective should not be to eliminate it completely. Your objective should be to reduce it as much as possible. When you've finished the steps I describe here, you'll be a better, more active writer.

Recognize Why Passive Voice Is a Problem

Passive voice is everywhere, but it's especially common when people want "something to be done." They write a report saying what needs to happen but hide who has to do the work. If you try to act on a recommendation like this, you immediately get stuck. You can't figure out who's supposed to do what.

To illustrate this, here are five sentences from a report that some folks at the University of Massachusetts wrote to analyze the cost and challenges of mounting the Olympic Games in Boston, with the passive constructions highlighted in bold. Imagine for a moment that you were helping to make this decision. Would these sentences help you or just obscure who is responsible? (If you want a chuckle, add "by zombies" after the verb in each one to convince yourself that they're passive.)

[These are] issues that **will need to be closely monitored** in order to ensure the public sector **is protected** from extensive financial commitments. [Who is supposed to monitor the issues? Who is protecting the public sector? Somebody in government, but they're not saying who.]

The operations expenditures for the Boston 2024 Olympics **are estimated** to create or support nearly 34,000 direct jobs during the year of the Olympics. [Who is estimating? The authors of the report. Be especially wary of the words "expected" or "estimated" as they're meaningless unless you know whose expectations and estimates we're talking about.]

[A]fter the Olympics, the Olympic Stadium site and Olympic Boulevard **could be developed** into seven million square feet of mixed use residential and commercial space. [Who will develop them? Unless somebody is willing to make a real estate investment, this passage is irrelevant.]

To date, using insurance to protect a host city from cost overruns **has not been used** extensively. [In this case, the answer to

"Who will do this?" is "Nobody." That doesn't give the reader much confidence.]

[Local Olympic Committee] revenue sources **cannot be used** to construct permanent or legacy projects for a region. Permanent construction associated with the Olympic Games **would be paid for** using other funding sources. [Budgets and passives are a bad combination. If you need to spend money, you need to know where it's coming from.]

Raise Your Awareness of Passive Voice

You write passive sentences because you read so many of them. Academic papers, news articles, and nearly everything else you read online are rife with passive voice. Passive sounds sort of sophisticated because it creates distance between the writer and the reader. Consciously or unconsciously, you've picked that up. Unfortunately, that distance also creates confusion.

In the WOBS Writing Survey, 32% of the business writers said that excessive use of the passive voice was frequently a problem in what they read, while 25% admitted it was frequently a problem in what they wrote.

The easiest way to become aware of passive voice is to give a draft of something you're writing to a good editor once you're at the paragraph- and line-editing stage. Have the editor highlight all the passive sentences.

I once edited a very smart analyst who didn't realize how bad his passive habit was. After marking up the first two cases of passive voice in his draft, I added this comment: "I'm going to ask you to slap yourself each time you write a passive voice sentence." For the rest of the document, I just marked each passive sentence and added the comment "Slap." In a 5-page document, he needed to slap himself about 30 times. Since then, he has become highly sensitive to the unconscious use of passive voice in his writing.

Even if you don't slap yourself, when you get the document back from your editor, you may be depressed. Don't be. That feeling of nausea is natural in the awareness stage. It gets a lot easier from here.

If you don't have a friendly editor, be aware that Microsoft Word will highlight passive voice for you, as will online tools like Grammarly. If you look for forms of "to be" with past tense verbs (actually, past participles), you'll spot a lot of them. Even so, I think a live editor is more helpful to coach you as you're learning to raise your awareness.

Reconsider Your Habit

Once you've gotten past the nausea, examine your passives. Why did you write them? What were you trying to hide? The reasons are not always the same. Consider these examples and the corresponding reasons (passives in bold).

> The puzzle of why big firms exhibit such innovative inertia **was placed into** a theoretical framework by Clayton Christensen in his pioneering book *The Innovator's Dilemma*. [The writer habitually writes in academic language. (From a book about the Internet.)]

A white paper **is considered to be** a standard marketing tool today. [The writer is unable or unwilling to present the research to back up this vague, unsupported statement. (From a web page.)]

Healthcare **is being transformed** to deliver care and services in a person-centered manner and **is increasingly provided** through community and home-based services. [The writer apparently doesn't want to talk about whose job it is to transform healthcare or who provides services. (From a government report.)]

While many passives are just lazy writing, fear is also a causative factor. You either don't want to say who's responsible for something or don't want readers to blame you. Writing these sentences in active voice is an act of courage, and one your readers will respect.

Rewrite Passive Sentences

Fixing passives sounds easy. Check that verb. Ask yourself who is placing, considering, and transforming. When you've answered the question, rewrite the sentence with that person or entity as the subject. But sometimes it's not so simple, as you can see from the following rewrites of the previous examples:

Clayton Christensen, in his pioneering book *The Innovator's Dilemma*, created a theoretical framework that solves the puzzle of why big firms exhibit such innovative inertia.

White papers are highly effective marketing tools that drive leads and boost email sign-ups.

We are experiencing a healthcare transformation. Healthcare providers increasingly deliver care and services in a person-centered manner in community and home-based services.

Rewriting passive voice makes you think harder about what you're saying. It may require research to prove an unsupported statement. You may need to rethink the sentence altogether. After careful consideration, you may decide to retain the passive sentence if you feel the object being acted on is more important than the actor. If you decide to keep it, make sure you've done so consciously, not just because you don't feel like figuring out the actor in the sentence.

Retrain Your Brain Around Active Voice

If you want to maintain the value of what you've learned, put passive checking into the line-edit stage of every piece of writing you do. Look for "is," "are," "can," "could," "have," "has," and "ought" in your writing, and ask if the sentences that include them are passive. This helps sharpen your "passive detector." Do it enough, and you'll learn to catch yourself as you're writing.

I also recommend going back to your editor/coach from time to time. They'll remind you where you're going wrong and help keep your passive detector properly calibrated.

7

Replace Jargon

Jargon is extremely useful. It makes writers seem like sophisticated insiders. Unfortunately, it makes life much harder for readers. Remember the Iron Imperative—that you must treat the reader's time as more valuable than your own? Jargon accomplishes the opposite: it clearly communicates that you think you are more important than the reader.

Let's look at an example. This is the first half of a press release that Oracle, a large technology company, published to announce a new version of a "business intelligence" product. The main purpose of the release is to help technology journalists, analysts, and others who follow the company's products to understand the value of the features in the new version. I've highlighted the jargon in bold.

Oracle Business Intelligence 12c Helps Organizations Boost Their **Digital Transformation** Through **Agile Visual Analytics** Major Release Delivers Unmatched Levels of Visual Simplicity, **Business Agility** and **Scalable Performance** Redwood Shores, Calif.—Nov 12, 2015

Oracle today announced the general availability of Oracle Business Intelligence 12c (BI 12c), designed to deliver an entirely new experience for blending and visually analyzing any data in an **enterprise-scale analytics platform**. The foundation of Oracle's analytics offerings, Oracle BI 12c allows people across the organization to **leverage** a single **integrated platform** for self-service, **visual data discovery** and quickly find answers to pressing business questions while in the office or on the go.

Analytics offerings today force organizations to make a difficult choice between **business agility** and **enterprise scale**: Desktop solutions offer **agile visual analytics** but are limited to user-managed or departmental data; traditional **BI** solutions offer **scalable performance** on IT-managed data, but compromise **agile self-service** and **time-to-value**. Only Oracle BI 12c delivers both in a no-compromise, modern platform that empowers people with stunning **visual analytics** as well as **curated dashboards** and analysis across personal, departmental and enterprise data. Oracle BI 12c advances the **state of the art** with an **integrated platform** delivering **self-service visual analytics**, a re-imagined **user experience**, **optimized in-memory processing**, built-in advanced analytics and simplified administration.

At best, a piece of writing like this accomplishes nothing except to confuse readers. At worst, it alienates readers and generates frustration and resentment.

Jargon spreads like a nasty mold across everything we write. And yet, the people who write it are trying hard to communicate; they're often so deep into the jargon habit that they don't see what's wrong. For example, 54% of the business writers in the WOBS Writing Survey said that excessive jargon is frequently a problem in what they read, but only 24% think it's problematic in what they write.

Let's take a look at why jargon happens and how you can fix it.

Jargon Springs from Insider Bias

In his writing book *The Sense of Style*, Steven Pinker describes the "Curse of Knowledge." It's what happens when smart people write about a topic that they know a lot about. Experts become so immersed in the areas of their expertise that they forget that most of their readers lack this knowledge. That's one reason why the press release writers at Oracle feel comfortable writing about "agile visual analytics"—because whatever that means, it is the product that their marketers and engineers are talking about all day long.

The problem is that when you write in jargon, you effectively divide the world into two groups. One is the insider group—the people who, along with you, know what these special words mean. The other, much larger, group is the world outside your bubble. That other group likely includes most of your customers and many of your employees. The more jargon you use, the more you are alienating large groups of people who should be reading and understanding what you write. You make them feel ignorant because they *are* ignorant; they don't know your secret code. Some of them will work hard to figure it out, but most will just give up on you and whatever you're trying to get across.

Call it insider bias—writing as if you were part of a small club that unfortunately excludes many of your readers. Here are some of the reasons that writers fall victim to insider bias:

- **Precision.** Writers want to use precise (but uncommon) language rather than more common, informal terminology (Oracle's "in-memory processing").
- **Efficiency.** Writers seek shortcuts: terminology that encompasses complex concepts in a few words ("visual data discovery").
- **Corporate cheerleading.** If the boss has defined the strategy around some special term, of course you want to use it to show you're on board ("business agility").
- **Inflation.** Big words sound impressive—they make a big noise, even if they communicate little ("state of the art").

In contrast to passive voice, which is just a habit, people write jargon to look and sound smarter. They don't. As Phil Simon, author of *Message Not Received*, reminded me, Albert Einstein once said, "If you can't explain it simply, you don't understand it well enough." Readers appreciate it if you prioritize clarity over sounding impressive.

Rewriting Jargon into Plain English

The first thing to change is your attitude. Do you think that writing in direct, informal language makes you seem too simplistic? The opposite is true. Let's take a look at two strategy statements. Here's one from a healthcare consultant:

> **System-level competition** is a new model for strategy in a **globally-linked**, information-oriented society. This is a methodology for strategic innovation that blends system design and

management, **ecosystem-centered business strategy,** and applications from **complex adaptive systems research.**

Compare it to this mission statement from Google:

Google's mission is to organize the world's information and make it universally accessible and useful.

Google's technology underpinnings are pretty sophisticated. This is not a dumb company, and the people working there are pretty clever. Google's founders Larry Page and Sergey Brin were smart enough to realize that a mission statement written in plain language is more effective. They don't need to puff themselves up with jargon. Neither do you.

Once you realize this, you can give yourself permission to rewrite whatever you're working on in plain language. That means looking at what you've written and asking, "Can a broad audience actually understand this?" If not, rewrite it using words and concepts anyone can understand. Here are some examples with the jargon highlighted:

Original (from an email about healthcare information strategies for America):

The **critical infrastructure** of the national health, healthcare, research, and human services **information supply chain** must be governed with a commitment to open and unbiased exchange, organized and operated for the public good.

Rewrite:

We will build a framework for health data sharing. Government, healthcare, and research entities will build it together.

Original (from a Johnson & Johnson job description):

The Area Vice President, Enterprise Customers will develop and manage a **sustainable strategic relationship** that transforms the **current commercial model** by creating joint value that results in the ongoing reduction of costs, **continuous process improvement**, growth and profitability for both partners with the ability to **export key learnings**.

Rewrite:

You'll show key enterprise customers the benefits of working with us and share what you learn.

Yes, my rewrites leave things out, but shorter is better. The desire to throw every possible jargon-laden concept into the text creates prose that's just for show, not for communication. You're better off communicating something real and simple than attempting and failing to get every possible idea into your copy.

To Write Jargon-Free Prose, Visualize Your Audience

Why not skip the rewriting step and just write clearly in the first place? Here's the trick.

Before you start, clearly visualize your audience. Is it a small-business person—maybe the owner of a hair salon? Is it an engineer who writes in Java? Is it all the customer service reps in your department? If you imagine *average* readers—not the smartest ones you know—and think of explaining whatever you're trying to get across to them, you'll be in the right mindset.

Then write a few simple, direct statements that, taken together, get across what you're trying to say. If you're communicating to the customer service reps, it might look like this:

A new software release of our product is going out this weekend.

New releases typically generate a lot of calls.

You need to familiarize yourself with the details of the update before you come in on Monday.

It's going to be stressful, but I'm counting on you to balance efficiency and politeness.

Please let me know if you're receiving calls or emails that indicate a more pervasive problem.

If you start by writing these simple statements in direct language, then you'll put yourself in the right frame of mind as you fill in the rest of the content.

Using Jargon Properly

It's understandable why people cling to their jargon. Whatever area you work in, there are some terms you just can't live without. Lawyers have to talk about liability and indemnification.

Manufacturers need to discuss outsourcing. Biologists need to talk about DNA. You wouldn't get very far without useful terms like these.

Even so, it is the proliferation of specialized terminology that turns the efficient use of a few key terms into a thicket of jargon that you can't hack through without a machete.

So here are three rules of thumb for when you *can* use jargon:

1. You can use terms that everyone in your audience knows. Just recognize that you're excluding people who don't know those terms. When people who sell consulting write about RFPs, most of the people they're communicating with know that means "request for proposal"—they get a pass on that term.
2. Where a term has a specific, legally required definition, define it and use it. For example, the word "disclaimer" has a specific legal meaning that makes it mandatory in some situations.
3. If there's a term you want to use throughout a document, define it up front. That's what I did in this chapter with "insider bias." But keep these "magic words" to a minimum. If you're only going to use an acronym once, why bother defining the acronym and using it? Just substitute a simpler term.

That's it. If you can't fit your jargon into one of these three exceptions, then replace it. You'll look smarter, and your readers will *feel* smarter.

8

Eliminate Weasel Words

You should generally eliminate most qualifiers from your writing, because they make you come off a bit wimpy and uncertain.

That sounds pretty lame, doesn't it? Here's what I should have said:

Weasel words—qualifiers like "very" and "generally"—make you, the writer, feel better at the expense of clarity and boldness. Prune them mercilessly.

That's appropriately direct.

In this chapter, I'll describe what weasel words are and how they destroy good writing. Then I'll explain how you can remove them without removing all the subtlety from your writing.

Why Weasel Words Are a Problem

Let's start with a definition.

A weasel word is an adjective, adverb, or noun that indicates quantity or intensity but lacks precision.

Grammatically, these words are typically called qualifiers or intensifiers. Here are some common weasel words: "most," "many," "few," "rarely," "millions," "cheap," "countless." I call them weasel words because they're the words that writers use to make flimsy generalizations that are not provable or defensible. And once I sensitize you to them, you'll see them everywhere.

For example, let's take a look at an article that Pat Gelsinger, CEO of the technology company VMware, contributed to the *Wall Street Journal* in 2015. Here are some excerpts from his article, which he wrote to show how VMware can help corporate chief information officers (CIOs) (weasel words shown in bold):

> Though **some** [CIOs] remain stuck in a "keep the lights on and stick to the budget" mindset, **many** now embrace the role of service provider, building and supporting **burgeoning** portfolios of IT services. **Still others** are emerging as strategists and decision-makers—a logical step for individuals who, after all, know more about technology than anyone else on the CEO's staff. . . . Today, the Internet and cloud can offer startups the infrastructure they need to create new applications and **potentially** reach **billions** of customers—all at a **low** cost. . . . Moreover, the ability to innovate **rapidly and affordably** is not the exclusive purview of tech startups. **Most** companies with traditional business models **probably** already have **a few** radical developers on staff.

The qualifiers in this article create the impression of content, but in fact say nothing. How many CIOs are embracing the role of service provider? How many are strategists? Can they reach their customers, or is this just potential? How low is "low cost"?

When a single sentence includes "most," "probably," and "a few," you know it's bullshit. No hard-nosed businessperson would make a decision based on that. Not only does this passage say nothing, it marks the CEO of VMware as a man who can't marshal facts to defend his perspective. It's worse than no statement at all.

Even words that sound strong—like "burgeoning" and "very"—actually weaken statements. As Steven Pinker points out in *The Sense of Style*, "If I'm wondering who pilfered the petty cash, it's more reassuring to hear *Not Jones; he's an honest man* than *Not Jones; he's a very honest man*. . . . As soon as you add an intensifier, you're turning an all-or-none dichotomy into a graduated scale."

If qualifiers make you sound like a wimp, why do people use them? Because of fear and laziness. It's bold to say "I'm sure you have radical developers on staff." Of course, you can't be certain. So you hedge and say "Most companies probably have a few radical developers on staff." The weaker your argument, the more you hedge. The problem is: we can see you hedging. Your qualifiers weaken your argument.

Esther Schindler, the experienced writer I introduced in chapter 1, has written hundreds of controversial pieces. As she explains, "You must take the emotion out of it. It's 'just the facts ma'am.' Especially when you are unsure of yourself, take out the 'I think' and 'It seems to me.' Say things with authority and people really do respond to that. Never explain or apologize."

The other reason writers use weasel words is to avoid the necessary research to get precise answers. It's easy to write that "the Internet and cloud can give you the potential to reach billions of customers at low cost." To be precise, you would have to say something like this: "There are 3 billion Internet users on the planet. In a typical company, Internet and cloud technologies mean that with an investment of less than $8 million, the average Fortune 1000 company can reach all of them." Of course, to say that, you'd have to do research on the number of Internet users and the average costs of Internet commerce for large companies. That's work. Making generalizations is easier; you just type them and no one can disprove them.

The image of the writer as a weasel creates shame, and that's why I use it. I want you to hate qualifiers and do everything you can to eliminate them.

How to Eliminate Weasel Words

Here's how weasel words get into your writing: You want to make a statement, but then you realize that you're not sure it's completely true. So you throw in a weasel word or three and feel comfortable you've covered your ass.

I want you to take a different path. When you want to write a general statement, write it as boldly as you can. Eliminate adverbs, wimpy adjectives, and vague quantities like "millions" and "many." Replace them with the boldest statements you can make, with actual numbers, or with specifics. Don't tell us that *many* people do something, tell us *which* people do it.

Let's look at some examples. Here's an excerpt from a letter that United Airlines' new CEO, Oscar Munoz, who took over when the previous CEO left in the wake of a scandal, sent to frequent flyers:

> I am excited about the incredible opportunity that the
> United team has to improve the travel experience essential

to the vitality of global business and to the personal lives of millions of people.

The words "incredible" and "millions" are weasel words, and "essential" is suspect, too. This passage comes off as overgeneralized corporate bullshit. To rewrite, just remove the weasel words or replace them with actual numbers.

> I am excited about the opportunity to improve your travel experience. I know that United Airlines is vital to the global business and personal travel that led you to take 140 million trips with us last year.

(That "140 million" came directly from United Airlines' online fact sheet; it took me 15 seconds to look it up.)

Here's a statement from presidential candidate Bernie Sanders's website, regarding the Black Lives Matter movement:

> A growing number of communities do not trust the police and law enforcement officers have become disconnected from the communities they are sworn to protect.

This doesn't really quantify the problem; "a growing number" is a typical political generalization. But the quantity isn't relevant anyway. Here's a restatement that speaks honestly about these communities:

> In communities where people don't trust the police, law enforcement officers lack a connection with those they are sworn to protect.

Lastly, remember that you can't fight off quantitative arguments with weasel words. In 2015, the video producer Hank Green wrote a popular blog post (3,281 people recommended it) in which he accused Facebook of lying, cheating, and stealing in the way it reported views of videos on Facebook. Green's post was full of statistics. Facebook product manager Matt Pakes responded to defend how Facebook counted native videos on its site compared to links to videos on other sites, but his defense included no numbers at all. Here's a typical sentence from Pakes's response:

> [P]eople tend to interact slightly less with non-native video, and the posts get less engagement. Native video posts with auto-play tend to see better engagement, more watch time and higher view counts.

If Facebook wants to retain credibility here, it must share its statistics, not talk about what "tends to" happen. For example, it would be far more effective if Pakes said something like this:

> People interact 15% less with nonnative video, and the posts get 20% fewer likes and shares. When viewing the same video in different formats, 40% more viewers watch native video posts with autoplay, and they watch for an average of 30 seconds longer.

(I made these numbers up; Pakes would have to substitute the actual data.)

Finally, let me answer one inevitable question. Must you eliminate *every* weasel word? No. If you're making a comparison, you'll need to say "less" or "more." If you're labeling an explosive, you'll want to note that it's "extremely unstable." But as with the other bad writing habits I've railed against, I want to sensitize you to weasel words so you'll notice them and prune as many of them as possible.

How to Cover Your Ass Without Using Weasel Words

People use weasel words to cover their asses. If you say "most customers are happy," then when an unhappy customer comes along, you can say you warned people.

The thing to recognize is, this doesn't work. If you've made a generalization, people will recognize it (and hold you responsible for it), even if you've carved out exceptions by saying "generally" or "for the most part" or whatever your preferred weasel word is.

Here's a rule of thumb for how to deal with those exceptions:

- If you're afraid of generalizing—if you think there's a good chance you're wrong—then don't generalize.
- If you think the exceptions are rare and not worth considering, go ahead and make a direct statement. Your readers will hold you responsible regardless of whether you said the exceptions happen "rarely" or didn't mention them at all, so you might as well be bold.
- If the exceptions are important enough to consider, write about them explicitly. ("Except for those with incomes exceeding $500,000, our investors renew at a 95% rate.")
- Where you can, use statistics to quantify how true a generalization is.

Together, Passive Voice, Jargon, and Weasel Words Cloud Writing

In the last three chapters, I've hit three bad writing habits that tend to go together: passive voice, jargon, and weasel words. Together, they're clear signifiers of bullshit. Writers use them to avoid responsibility for what they're writing. All of them make writing dense and hard to read, so they reduce the meaning ratio. They all make life harder for readers, violating the Iron Imperative. They're difficult habits to kick, but once you start noticing them, you're on your way to effective writing.

If you want to replace muddy writing with clarity, there's no better place to start than with these three signifiers of lazy, fearful writing. Cut your use of these three classes of bullshit by 90% and what's left will be active, clear, and bold. Isn't that how you'd like people to think of you?

9

Be Direct

Perhaps reading this book has made you uncomfortable. There's a reason for that.

I've been very clear about what I want you to do. As you read, you recognize that you have a choice to make. You can change your writing and do as I suggest or not, but you can't easily just nod your head and go "hmm" and do nothing.

I did that by using the pronouns "you" and "I" in my writing. Instead of describing a situation, I'm giving advice. If I were part of an organization, I would have used "we" as well, which adds a dimension to the directness.

To stand out, your business writing needs to make a direct connection between the writer and the reader. "You," "I," and "we" make that connection. A simple change of pronouns forces you to think clearly about what you're saying.

To Write with "You," Visualize Your Readers

In chapter 6, I told you to eliminate passive voice by visualizing your readers. The next step is to write directly to them using the word "you."

You can't write "you" unless you have a clear idea of your audience. If you don't know who you're writing for and what you want them to do, why bother writing at all? So prepare yourself to be direct by identifying the "who" you're writing for—your boss, the whole sales department, or all your customers.

You extend this directness by talking about "your boss," "your financial commitments," or anything else that uses the possessive form.

The "you" is also implicit in commands. When I say "Eliminate weasel words," you know who I'm talking to: it's you.

It can be a little scary to always be telling people what to do. What if you're just describing a situation? Perhaps you're just writing about how "millennials connect on social media" or that "our sales are up 15% this quarter." But there's no point in writing about this without some sort of analysis or recommendation ("Let's invest in a social media hire," or "We should make sure the new product team gets appropriate credit"). Without "you," there's no advice. And without any advice, the reader asks, why did I spend time reading this?

If you're writing to an audience within your organization, there is some nuance to this. When you write to subordinates, it's appropriate to be quite direct ("Here's what you should do"). When writing to colleagues or superiors, you must make your recommendations a bit more respectful ("Based on my research, here's what I think would be your/our best course of action"). But don't be afraid to make recommendations, even to those higher up. Managers find it frustrating when a staffer presents information without any context on why it's important. If your bosses don't need to act on it, why are you bothering them in the first place?

As for communication aimed at customers or other business partners, you pretty much have to include "you" in that communication. As in "You should improve your insurance coverage before it snows again," or "You ought to consider a real estate investment." Or give a command, like "Save money now."

By the way, the time to visualize audiences is *before* you start to write. I describe how to do that in chapter 13.

Get over Your Fear of "I"

Your writing teachers told you not to use "I" in writing. This is because juvenile writers end up repeating "I think" and "I believe," making their writing into a sort of personal narrative. College writing trains you to analyze what you read, and you're not supposed to substitute your judgment for that of the experts you're analyzing. That's why "I" seems so jarring in academic writing.

In business, the opposite is true. Whatever you write, it reflects your integrity and judgment. You should take responsibility. The alternative is weak: the classic passive voice dodge.

Which writer would you rather hear from: the one who writes, "I think we're ready to pick a supplier," or the one who writes, "Now a supplier can be chosen"?

In my WOBS Writing Survey, 49% of business writers complained that what they read was frequently less effective because it was not direct enough. But only 8% complained about business writing being too informal. Most of us (at least the men) have shed our ties. Now it's time for us to embrace our pronouns.

As I described in chapter 3, women are more likely to have challenges with being direct *in person* than men. But interestingly, in my survey, women and men were almost equally likely to report problems with directness in their own writing—36% of women reported that problem, compared with 38% of men. For women seeking to be bolder in their communication, learning to use "I" and "you" in their writing is an easy win.

Look, they're going to blame you if you make the wrong recommendation anyway. Why not use "I" and own up to your responsibility?

Use "We" to Show You're Part of a Team

Sometimes you're speaking for a group. For example, you may be speaking for the company: "We will always respond to your service requests within one day." Or for your collaborators: "We have analyzed the consumer data, and we believe that the market is open to purchasing at a 20% higher price point." If you can't use "I," use "we."

Beware the trap of the indeterminate "we," though. When you write, "We're uncomfortable with issuing a legal threat," whom are you speaking for? A committee? A department? Don't write "we" unless you've made it clear which team you're speaking for. Otherwise you sound like royalty ("We find your offer acceptable, and yes, we will marry you").

How to Rewrite for Directness with Pronouns

Before you can improve a piece of writing with these pronouns, write down who the audience is (who is "you") and whom you're speaking for (who is "we"). Then blaze ahead, transforming bland statements about what's happening or what needs to happen. Rewrite, telling what "I" or "we" think "you" should do. Or write commands telling the reader what to do.

Let's see how this works in practice. The examples I show here are pretty laden with bullshit and waste the reader's time. And that's no coincidence; when you haven't got a clear idea of who's writing and who's listening, you're bound to be writing crap. Answering these questions is the first step on the way to clear writing.

For example, here's part of the company overview from the Avaya corporate website:

> Avaya is a recognized innovator and leading global provider of solutions for customer and team engagement. The company provides technologies for unified communications and collaboration, contact center and customer experience management, and networking, along with related services to large enterprises, midmarket companies, small businesses and government organizations around the world. Avaya Engagement Solutions bring people together with the right information at the right time in the right context, helping to enable a higher level of engagement between customers, teams, employees and partners to improve efficiency and quickly address critical business challenges. Designed to be highly scalable, reliable, secure and flexible, these solutions help reduce costs and simplify management while providing a platform for next-generation engagement and collaboration.

This obviously has problems with jargon and weasel words ("recognized," "leading"). But you can clear up those problems by writing directly with "you" and "we." In this example, "you" refers to customers, and "we," to the company. Avaya needs to figure out what it does for these customers and then write about it simply. So the rewrite looks like this:

> At Avaya, we provide communication and networking technologies to businesses and government groups of all sizes. We make teams and partnerships more efficient. Our solutions help you cut costs and simplify management.

Notice how the first sentence defines what "we" means (Avaya) and what "you" refers to ("businesses and government groups of all sizes"). From there, it's a lot easier to rewrite the description in terms of what "we" do for "you."

Let's look at another example. This comes from the business development job description for Johnson & Johnson that I mentioned in chapter 7:

> The successful candidate will be the key leader and customer advocate working closely with the Strategic Account and Sales Leaders across J&J to facilitate execution against strategic account terms, interface with account management executives and sales leaders enterprise-wide to align and deliver high quality service and value, ensure coordinated execution of customer solutions through clinical and economic services and programs, and facilitate the management of and coordinate direct sales personnel and resources. They will contribute to positively driving business model change and executing against innovative approaches in the new environment, contribute to the development of enterprise account model that

will change the way J&J operates in the marketplace, and will hold accountability for effective, creative contract and agreement leadership working across different sectors of the organization.

Again, the description is full of bullshit. But you can clear the bullshit by asking what the candidate ("you") will do for the company ("we" or "us").

You'll work with sales to coordinate our resources to make sure we deliver what we promise. You'll take advantage of what you learn to develop new ways for the different parts of Johnson & Johnson to work together to serve customers.

Some would argue that these descriptions are too informal. But formality serves little purpose when it interferes with clarity. Google is just as complex a company as Avaya or Johnson & Johnson, but take a look at how simply Google describes its number one priority:

Focus on the user and all else will follow. Since the beginning, we've focused on providing the best user experience possible. Whether we're designing a new Internet browser or a new tweak to the look of the homepage, we take great care to ensure that they will ultimately serve *you*, rather than our own internal goal or bottom line. Our homepage interface is clear and simple, and pages load instantly. Placement in search results is never sold to anyone, and advertising is not only clearly marked as such, it offers relevant content and is not distracting. And when we build new tools and applications, we believe they should work so well you don't have to consider how they might have been designed differently.

Google proudly talks about what "we" do for "you." So can you. And you'll stand out by doing it.

10

Use Numbers Wisely

Words lie. Numbers don't.

Numbers are precise, reliable, and persuasive. Except when they aren't.

Let's look at the example of Bernadette McMenamin, the CEO of the Australian organization Child Wise, who really wants to prevent the sexual exploitation of children. In a 2008 article in the *Australian* newspaper, she wrote:

> Child pornography is one of the fastest growing online businesses generating approximately $US3 billion ($3.43 billion) each year. It is estimated that 100,000 commercial websites offer child pornography and more than 20,000 images of child pornography are posted on the internet every week.

One hundred thousand child pornography sites is shocking. But is it true? By now, you know enough to be suspicious of any sentence that begins with the passive "It is estimated." So who estimated it?

The estimated number of child pornography sites appeared in a report by the US-based National Center for Missing and Exploited Children in 2005. They apparently got it from the Royal

Canadian Mounted Police (RCMP), who published it earlier that year. The RCMP got it from US Customs and Border Protection. (Apparently, the North American Free Trade Agreement encourages swapping of dubious statistics freely across the US-Canadian border.) Kevin Delli-Colli, who was a Customs Service official, gave the estimate to a reporter for the *Christian Science Monitor* in 2000. Where he got it, who knows.

As a parent, I hate child pornography as much as anyone. In fact, I hate it twice as much as Kevin Delli-Colli, the US Customs and Border Protection, the Royal Canadian Mounted Police, the Center for Missing and Exploited Children, and Bernadette McMenamin. I hate it so much that I am going to say that there are 200,000 child pornography sites. So we should dedicate twice as much effort to getting rid of it.

What's that? You say I can't just make up numbers?

The Internet is full of made-up numbers. Carl Bialik studied this phenomenon for nine years as the Numbers Guy columnist for the *Wall Street Journal*. He's watched numbers like the 100,000 child porn sites ricochet across the Internet, shorn of their sources. For many writers, he says, "the incentive is going to be: let's find the number that makes the case most compellingly." Not the number that's actually accurate.

Your readers know this is a problem. In the WOBS Writing Survey of over 500 business-writing professionals, 24% said the material they read was frequently less effective because of poor or inappropriate use of statistics. While this is fewer than the number who complained about writing that was too long or poorly organized, that's still a lot of people who have problems with statistics.

Don't just pick that number up off the street. Who knows where it's been?

In this chapter, I'll show you how to fairly and appropriately use numbers with a provenance, in context, and with appropriate precision.

Provide Context to Make Numbers Meaningful

On September 1, 2015, the Dow Jones Industrial Average dropped 470 points.

How bad is that? Unless you have something to compare it to, the number has no meaning.

The Dow was at 16,528 when the day started. It ended the day at 16,058. That means it dropped 2.84% in one day. If you had $1,000 invested in a Dow index fund, you lost $28.40. While nobody likes to lose the price of a nice lunch, it won't make you broke.

How about some historical perspective? Of all the Dow price drops from its inception through the end of 2015, this was the nineteenth worst. It's not nearly as bad as the 778 points the Dow shed seven years earlier, on September 29, 2008. That was the start of the Great Recession.

But in terms of what these drops mean for your investments, it's percentage that matters, not points. The Dow lost 508 points on October 19, 1987, "Black Monday," close to the same magnitude as the September 1, 2015, drop I've been discussing. But in 1987, that drop meant that 23% of the value of the index vaporized in one day. That's vertiginous. (I know I'll never forget it; I owned stock in a company that had planned to go public that fall, but after Black Monday, the public offering never happened.)

In fact, that 470-point drop on September 1, 2015, was not

even in the top 20 for percentage losses in one day. If you panic when the Dow drops 470 points, this would have been your second panicky moment in a two-week period—with lots more to come.

Now we have context. Without context, 470 is just a number. And the same is true of *every* number.

Citing a number without anything to compare it to deprives your readers of the information they need to make a decision. Their response is, "Huh?" They don't "get it." Numbers without context waste the reader's time, violating the Iron Imperative.

Here are some more examples lacking context. Let's start with this prediction from Gartner, Inc.

> We predict, for example, that in 2016 spending on new Internet of things (IoT) hardware will exceed $2.5 million a minute. And, as mind boggling as that number is, it pales in comparison with the corresponding prediction that, by 2021, 1 million IoT devices will be purchased and installed every single hour.

Boggling the mind with stats doesn't illuminate anything. How does this spending compare to other spending on hardware and other device installations? Is this 100 times what we spend now or twice that amount?

Now let's learn about streaming video from ReelSEO.com.

> According to the new [Nielsen] Total Audience Report, online video streaming viewers are growing online at an astonishing 60% per month pace this month, whereas TV has declined roughly 4%.

Growth rates are a common source of confusion. These two rates are not easily comparable. Without a base, any percentage is hard to comprehend, and in this case, there is no base for how many streaming viewers there are. And did TV decline 4% *per month*? I doubt it.

Be especially careful with press releases. Here's a paragraph in a release from HD Vest, a company that provides financial advisors, about its new software VestVision.

> Since its launch in August 2014, HD Vest–affiliated financial advisors have utilized VestVision to create nearly 8,000 investment plans for their clients, with 44 advisors creating their first VestVision-driven investment plan per month in 2015 on average.

Is the number of investment plans—8,000—a lot? How impressive is 44 plans per month? It turns out that HD Vest had 4,600 investment advisors when it made this statement. Now we know that 1% of them create new plans each month, and in total they've created around two plans per advisor. Not that impressive.

If you'd like to avoid the "huh?" factor, follow these rules to add context:

- **Always compare numbers to something familiar.** If, as the *Telegraph* wrote, British people spend an average of £800 a year on Christmas presents, how does that sum compare to their incomes or to the amount they spend on groceries every month?
- **Give us historical context.** How has the number you're citing changed? If you're reporting that your company now

has 250,000 customers, how many did it have at this time last year?

- **Don't publish growth rates without a base.** When I was an analyst, vendors were always telling me stuff like "Our revenues have grown 200% in the last year." That means nothing; if you brought in $100 last year, then the $300 you've generated this year isn't very impressive. Unless you cite both the growth and the base, your numbers lack the context to be credible.

Make the Case for Causality

America's spending on science is growing. We spent $18 billion in 1999, and, by 2009, that had risen to $30 billion.

Some people find overspending on science to be depressing, perhaps so depressing they want to hang themselves. In 1999, 5,000 Americans did just that. And in 2009, right along with the increase in science spending, the hangings increased to nearly 9,000.

In figure 5, you can see just how closely the two trends mirror each other. The correlation coefficient is about 99%.

What relates these two variables?

Nothing, of course. It's a coincidence. But we love patterns, so we see them even when they're not there.

Writers exploit this all the time, whether out of ignorance or bias. For example, which party is better for the US economy: Democrats or Republicans? Adam Hartung, a contributor to *Forbes*, says it's the Democrats because personal disposable income has grown nearly six times more under Democratic

FIGURE 5. The close correlation between science spending and hangings.

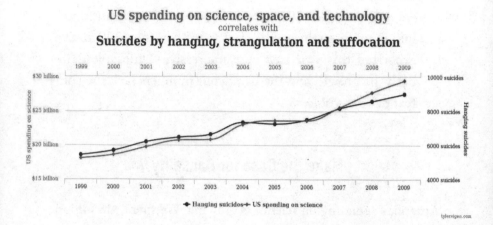

US spending on science, space, and technology
correlates with
Suicides by hanging, strangulation and suffocation

Chart by Tyler Vigen from his book *Spurious Correlations*, used by permission.

presidents. The *Economist*, on the other hand, explains that "the timing of Democratic presidents appears impeccable compared with Republicans—Mr. Clinton took office just as the technology sector began to boom, whereas George W. Bush could not get out before the financial crisis."

Causality in the economy is a bitch to prove. Congress and presidents have less influence than oil prices, Middle East wars, Eurozone instability, and Federal Reserve moves. Of course, that doesn't stop partisan writers from spinning it either way. Be skeptical of what you read.

And similarly, when it comes to causation, be careful what you write.

Why are your sales down? It could be that you changed sales models. Or it could be a new competitor, a change in the economy, or technology disruption. Or it could be the IT guy who re-jiggered your website and put the Buy button in the wrong color. It's very easy to say, "We changed our sales model, and sales dropped," but concurrent events don't always cause each other. (Should we blame those hanging deaths on science spending?)

Here's how to present causation responsibly in what you write:

- State your case. People need to know your perspective (and potential bias) up front.
- Cite your numbers, including context.
- Cite supporting evidence.
- Evaluate competing explanations.
- Explain how to test your conclusion.
- Explain what to do about what you've found.

Here's an example that might appear in an email:

To: Management Team
Subject: Our new sales model is causing a drop in sales

Folks, I've come to the conclusion that our new sales model is interfering with sales efficiency.

Here are the facts: In the last three months, sales of our flagship product are down 15%, from $4.0 million to $3.4 million. I've looked carefully into the cause. I spoke to ten salespeople, all of whom said that the new model adds time-consuming steps to their sales process and takes time away from selling.

Here's why I'm convinced that the model is the cause: during the same three-month period, the economy overall grew 1.0%, and, as you know, our sales generally track economic growth. The industry's sales as a whole grew 2.0% while our sales were dropping. Our competitors gained share without introducing new products or changing pricing. And our secondary product offering, FastTrack, which is not yet on the same sales model, didn't suffer the same sales drop.

I predict that we'll see the same sales drop for the three products that just went on the new model last month.

Assuming I'm right, we need to revamp the sales model immediately. I propose that we start a team to do that at our next management meeting.

Be Precise About Precision

A 2015 government poll of 2,700 people in Thailand revealed that "98.9% of respondents were satisfied and confident in the government's performance," according to the Associated Press. That's a curiously precise number.

This poll has a margin of error of 2%. What we've learned is that about one in a hundred Thais is sufficiently brave to express dissatisfaction, even though the government is under military rule. Reporting this to the nearest 0.1% is a lie because it implies a false level of precision.

The same problem happens in reverse—for example, when you read that the gross domestic product is rising at a 2% annual rate, even though the US Department of Commerce has carefully measured it at 2.0%. The extra zero matters in this case; 2.0% is less than 2.1% and greater than 1.9%.

Don't make this mistake in your business communication. Just because your spreadsheet or business information system tells you that the technical support team solved 75.33% of the 27,615 calls it received last month doesn't mean you actually have four digits of precision. Report the 75% and use that for comparisons. The numbers you report should be exactly as precise as the source material—and in this case, two digits of precision is far more likely than four.

Here's how to treat precision in your business writing:

- **Don't show more than three significant digits.** There's no point in reading the last digit of 75.33% or 7.533 billion unless you're a scientist weighing electrons or something similarly precise. (Exception: stock indexes and stock prices, which you can report exactly.)
- **Don't show more digits than you know.** If a survey has a margin of error of 3%, then round to the nearest percent, not the nearest tenth: 75% is the truth, while 75.3% is a lie. When you've calculated a result from other data, your calculated result should have no more digits of precision than the numbers you put in. If you know you have 23 million customers who together accounted for $1.42 billion in revenue, then the average customer generates $62, even if your spreadsheet tells you it's $61.739.
- **Cite growth rates of percentages properly.** Here's a quick quiz. Your market penetration—the percentage of all potential customers who buy your product—is 10.7%. Last year, it was 9.7%. By what percentage did your penetration grow? Two answers are correct. The statement "Penetration grew by 1.0 percentage points" is correct (10.7–9.7=1.0). And

"Penetration grew at a 10% rate" is also correct (1.0/9.7=10%, rounded to two significant digits). But "We grew penetration 1%" is wrong since it implies a growth rate.

Fight Bias

On November 23, 2015, *Breitbart* reported that Hillary Clinton would lose to any Republican candidate in a head-to-head battle. A Fox News poll of 1,016 registered voters revealed that Donald Trump would beat Hillary Clinton, 46% to 41%.

A few weeks later, *Alternet* reported that Clinton would beat any Republican on the ballot and would win by 47% to 41% over Trump, according to a Quinnipiac poll of 1,453 registered voters.

Did Clinton surge in popularity over two weeks? Not likely. In fact, previous polls from the same organizations showed similarly contradictory trends.

Breitbart is a conservative blog and Fox News is a conservative network. They highlight news favorable to conservatives. *Alternet* likes to report progressive news.

How could bias affect a poll? Before asking about voting matchups, Fox News first asked about Barack Obama's approval ratings and then asked, "How likely do you think it is that Islamic terrorists will try to launch an attack on US soil in the near future?" Such questions might easily change the state of mind of the voters in the poll.

We've all now grown used to potential bias in our media. But how does bias infect corporate communications?

The most pernicious form of bias within companies is confirmation bias. As the Emory University psychologist Scott Lilien-feld told the *Wall Street Journal,* "We're all mentally lazy. . . . It's simply easier to focus our attention on data that supports our hypothesis, rather than to seek out evidence that might disprove it." This manifests itself in the corporate world, where people develop an intuitive view of the causes and strategies they believe in and then collect statistics that prove their point.

I'm not counseling you to avoid having a point of view—as you've observed from the rest of this book, you've got to have one to stand out. But when it comes to numbers, you should be aware of where they're coming from and how that affects what they say. All research has biases, and all data collection has flaws. Go ahead and quote it, just don't convince yourself that everything that confirms your theory is right while everything that contradicts it is a fluke.

A great way to test yourself for bias is to make friends with someone who (respectfully) disagrees with you. They'll bring up the counterarguments and surface the statistics contrary to the way you think. This helps you to assess numbers objectively. And who knows—you might even change your mind once in a while.

Scrutinize the Methodology Behind Numbers

The United Way of Greater Saint Louis asks, "Did you know that the average middle class child is read to 1,000 hours before entering first grade, while the average low-income family only reads to their children an average of 25 hours?"

That's pretty amazing. But is it true? And where did those numbers come from?

As Carl Bialik points out, this number is a great example of statistics abuse. Bialik tracked the number down to Marilyn Jager Adams's 1990 book *Beginning to Read: Thinking and Learning About Print*. The 25 hours for low-income kids? That comes from a study of 22 low-income families. And the 1,000 hours? That's a sample of one: her own son.

This is the quadruple-whammy of misleading statistics. When it comes to methodology, here are four things that can render a number questionable, if not meaningless, and this statistic has all four:

1. **Is there a source you can check?** For the United Way of Greater Saint Louis, the answer is no. Unless somebody stands behind a stat, it's invalid. Statistics without sources spread like poison ivy across the web.

2. **If there is a source, is it methodologically sound?** Sound studies use concepts like statistical significance, random sampling, and comparison to control groups. This statistic has none of those qualities. The "methodology," such as it is, is unsupportable.

3. **What's the sample size?** Sample size determines the uncertainty of a number in a study. A study of 22 families is questionable. And a sample of one child, especially if the child is the researcher's son, is of no value whatsoever for comparison purposes.

4. **Is it up-to-date?** Adams reported her findings in 1990. The United Way of Greater Saint Louis cited it 21 years later, in 2011. Statistics have an expiration date. If I'm reporting smartphone behavior, anything older than nine

months is out of date. Children's reading statistics might change more slowly than that, but you certainly can't count on numbers from 1990 to reflect today's reality.

If the stats you cite have *any* of these four problems, we're going to have to revoke your license to use numbers.

To cite numbers properly, report the source and the date, and make sure you know the sample size if it's a study. And since your readers are online, include a link to the source so your readers can check it.

Here's an example of citing numbers properly, from the *Washington Post*:

[T]he share of income accounted for by the middle class has plummeted over the past 4½ decades [according to a recently released study by the Pew Research Center]. In 1970, middle-class households accounted for 62 percent of income; by 2014, it was just 43 percent. Meanwhile, the share held by those in upper-income households rose from 29 percent to 49 percent, eclipsing the middle class's share.

This article cites and links to fresh research from a respected nonprofit research firm, the Pew Research Center, based on a survey of 55,000 households from the US Bureau of Labor Statistics. Based on a sample that large, findings rounded to the nearest percent are certainly believable. By comparing numbers both across classes and over time, the writer has given us context to make sense of the data.

Some Final Words About Data

Throughout this book, I've been telling you to avoid weasel words like "very" and "many" and replace them, if possible, with numbers. Now I'm telling you to be very careful with numbers, questioning their sources, precision, meaning, context, and methodology.

You probably think you can't win here. Actually, you can. It's just going to take a little work.

Making business decisions is hard. You can help by communicating with numbers that you can back up and trust. A trustworthy worker reports trustworthy numbers; conversely, a worker who reports questionable numbers is suspect.

Checking your numbers before citing them is a pain in the ass. Do it anyway. Your integrity is on the line here. Check your data, because writing without bullshit depends on data that's not bullshit.

11

Reveal Structure

Prose sucks.

I've already told you to write shorter, put the best stuff up front, eliminate the wimpy words, and use pronouns to speak directly to the reader. Now it's time to think skeptically about the idea of words altogether.

Every paragraph that your reader reads, they're potentially losing interest. The more paragraphs, the greater the chance they won't make it to the end of what you've written.

Unless it's short, a piece of writing made of paragraphs looks uniform and therefore intimidating, especially on a narrow screen like a smartphone. Anything that's worth reading and is more than 300 words long has a structure of some kind. Reveal that structure, and you've given the reader some signposts. They see what's coming, and that it looks interesting.

That's why you need to mix up your text with headings, bullets, lists, tables, graphics, quotes, and links.

Get Over Your Bias Toward Paragraphs, Even in Short Documents

Remember those papers you wrote in college? They were made of paragraphs. You might have had a few section headings, but not necessarily. And if you wrote five-paragraph themes in high school, they were obviously made of paragraphs.

The newspaper and magazine articles you read are made of paragraphs, too.

But you're not writing for *Esquire* and you're not writing for your university professor. You're writing for an impatient business audience. You can impress them, not with your literary prose, but with your content and meaning. And those are a lot more accessible if you make your prose chunky, mixing in easily skimmable elements that reveal structure.

If you've read research reports, you've seen how this kind of information-dense writing can be effective. But I'm not just telling you to do it for reports and long documents.

Write bullets in your 250-word email to some colleagues. Put graphics in your marketing email. Add section heads to your blog post. And pop a chart into your Facebook post.

Modern tools make it easy to insert nuggets like these into your writing. You're not a Victorian novelist. So stop writing nothing but words, as if you're writing on a scroll with a quill pen. Real writers don't just type words; they mix in lots of goodies to keep the reader interested and enlightened.

It all comes back to the Iron Imperative: Treat the reader's time as more valuable than your own. Readers who can see the structure of what you've written know it's worth their time. Making navigation easy is part of your job.

Chunk Your Content with Headings, Bullets, and Lists

What you write always has a beginning, middle, and end. Break things up into chunks, then use headings to make those chunks easy to see. Within the chunks, use lists to create even more structure.

For example, consider the blog of customer experience expert Augie Ray. In August 2015, he wrote a controversial 3,300-word post about marketers' misguided use of social media. You could see the structure of his post in its title and three headings:

Burn It Down, Start from Scratch and Build a Social Media Strategy That Works
　　Destroying Social Media Marketing Myths With Data
　　Building Social Media Strategies With Data
　　Doing Social Media Right

The structure also continues under each of the subheads. The first section is written as a list of myths. And under the third heading, Ray uses bullets with bold leads to list out the steps in doing social media well:

Doing Social Media Right
　　Most companies are doing social wrong and have done it wrong from the beginning. The key to success is to stop most of what today passes for social media strategy and rebuild social plans from the ground up:
- **First, create and measure a new definition of WOM [Word of Mouth].** An individual who recommends your

brand based on their actual customer experience is gold; a customer who clicks the "heart" button on a pretty photo posted by your brand isn't even tin. . . . [*I've clipped out the rest of this bullet.*]

- **Toss out your social media scorecard immediately.** The first step to refocus social activities on what matters is to change what is measured. Stop rewarding employees or agencies for generating engagement that fails to deliver business benefit and start measuring what matters—changes in customer loyalty or consideration, positive and authentic Word of Mouth, inbound traffic that converts, quality lead acquisition and customer satisfaction. [*Section continues for five more similar bullets.*]

You can easily scan this post and focus on the parts that interest you. The headings and bolded bullets enable the post to function as its own table of contents.

To use this organizational technique in your own writing:

- **Insert headings as guideposts.** Your writing has a natural sequence, for example: identifying the problem, analyzing the options, making a recommendation. Create a descriptive heading for each element. If necessary, rewrite text to enable clear section boundaries. Even in an email or Facebook post, you can create pseudo headings with words in all caps, like ALTERNATIVES and RECOMMENDATION.
- **Create at most two head levels.** Only lawyers, legislators, and manual writers embrace organizational labels like "Section A.3.1.b." For the rest of us humans, try to stick to a single level of heads and sections. If sections get too long or you want

to reveal a second level of organization, include subheads and subsections. (For example, in this book, some chapters have one level of heading, and some have subheads as well.)

- **Embrace lists to ease navigation.** Any time you compare or describe three or more things, use a bulleted list. If it's in sequence, use a numbered list. Train yourself to put sentences, phrases, or words at the head of each list item in bold, as signposts. Lists now belong in anything nonfictional that people read, from press releases to software instructions. Look for words like "firstly" and "on the other hand" as clues that you've got prose that would be better written as a list.

Use Graphics as a Parallel Track for Meaning

David Armano, global strategy director for the agency Edelman, is an avid blogger who uses graphics to his advantage. For example, he began his October 2014 blog post called "Societal: The Third Dimension of Modern Day Brand Building" with an eye-catching graphic (see figure 6).

David Armano just thinks graphically—ideas and pictures form together in his mind. He explains, "As consumers of content become more literate visually, the role of graphics moves beyond simply illustrating the written word which accompanies a piece of content; it can become the thing that determines if people will actually stop what they are doing and pay attention to that content. It can also be the thing that not only grabs their attention, but causes a reader to share a written piece. Never before have visuals played such a critical role in writing."

FIGURE 6. Graphic by David Armano for a blog post on brand building.

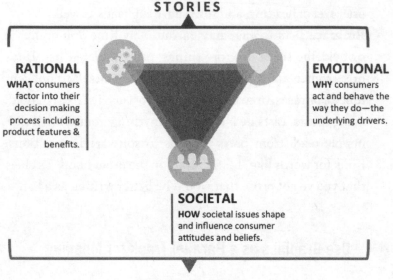

STORIES

RATIONAL
WHAT consumers factor into their decision making process including product features & benefits.

EMOTIONAL
WHY consumers act and behave the way they do—the underlying drivers.

SOCIETAL
HOW societal issues shape and influence consumer attitudes and beliefs.

EXPERIENCES

If you're trying to get across a complex idea and the words won't flow—or if there are just too many words—draw a picture. Brainstorm it on the whiteboard. Pull in somebody who's graphically talented if you want. But your graphical ideas don't need to be complex. Simple Venn diagrams, flow charts, or boxes with arrows can often do the job. For example, one day, as I was trying to explain to somebody that practice, experience, and editing are what you need to become a better writer, I came up with a simple chart (see figure 7).

That's as basic as it gets. But it gets the point across.

In addition to diagrams like this, you can include data graphics such as line charts, bar charts, and pie charts. (Use the tests

FIGURE 7. How to become a better writer.

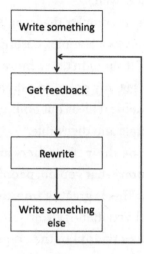

from the previous chapter to make sure that the data isn't bullshit.) You can build them simply with a tool like Microsoft PowerPoint, use more sophisticated drawing tools like Adobe Illustrator, or hire a designer to make them look great. (I'd write my own book on graphics without bullshit, but it already exists: Edward Tufte's *The Visual Display of Quantitative Information*.)

Once created, graphics pay endless dividends with their flexibility. You can paste them into emails, embed them in web pages and blog posts, attach them to tweets and Facebook posts, drop them into documents, and use them in presentations. But regardless of how you use graphics, remember three key things:

1. **Graphics and text are parallel ways of representing meaning.** The text and the graphics in a document should work together. With a diagram, you can show things that

would be hard to explain in text, but the text should still carry meaning as well.

2. **Keep it simple.** A complex diagram thwarts the reader just as effectively as a complex description. As David Armano says, "It shouldn't take more than a few seconds for a reader to 'get' my point, so I spend time not only identifying graphical ideas but boiling them down to something simple and digestible."

3. **Graphics escape their containers and roam the web freely.** No matter what you do, people will clip and share your graphics. This is great; it improves your reach. But make sure that you identify yourself, your web address, and your sources (if any) in the graphic, because it's going to burst forth from your document and go tearing across your company, or the open web, whether you like it or not.

Exploit the High Information Density of Tables

A table stands out from the text like a graphic but enables you to present structured content neatly, like a list. Tables deliver a lot of information in a small space. Just don't get carried away and try to stuff all your data into a single table.

Numerical tables with a dozen or so rows can deliver more precise information than a bar chart. Add a second column and you'll create a graphic that rewards further study.

Tables aren't only about numbers. Simple text tables can succinctly summarize what you've written. For example, when I did a blog post about writing that included a text table, people shared the table graphic across the web thousands of times (see figure 8).

If you're going to use tables, I have one caveat. Formatting tables is a pain in the ass. Unlike graphics, which will retain their graphical integrity when plunked into many different contexts, tables clipped from Microsoft Word, for example, don't maintain their column sizes and proportions when pasted into a web page. Don't waste time fiddling with formats. Just take a screen shot of the table and insert it into a different context as a graphic. (Text in table graphics isn't searchable, regrettably.)

FIGURE 8. Ten writing tips and the psychology behind them.

(bs) bernoff.com

Ten writing tips and the psychology behind them

Tip	Why it matters	Why you fail	How to fix
Write shorter.	Readers are impatient.	You just keep typing; it's easier than editing.	Edit out extraneous text.
Shorten your sentences.	Long sentences puzzle readers.	You tack on ideas as you're writing.	Break into shorter sentences.
Rewrite passive voice.	Passive hides true meaning.	You're insecure about what you're saying.	Make the actor the sentence's subject.
Eliminate weasel words.	Weasel words make statements wimpy.	You're afraid to be bold.	Cut weasel words; if you can't, cut the sentence.
Replace jargon with clarity.	Jargon makes readers feel stupid.	You think jargon sounds sophisticated.	Replace with plain English.
Cite numbers effectively.	Stats back up your point.	You think any number adds credibility.	Include both context and source for stats.
Use "I," "we," and "you."	Pronouns invite the reader to relate.	You're afraid of sounding informal.	Imagine the reader; write directly to her.
Move key insights up.	Bold statements retain attention.	You feel the need to "warm up" first.	Write bold openers; rewrite with each draft.
Cite examples.	Text without examples is boring.	You're too busy to do the research.	Plan to spend half your time on research.
Give us some signposts.	Readers want to know what's coming.	You're afraid of sounding pedantic.	After stating thesis, explain what's coming.

Created by Josh Bernoff, WOBS LLC

This work is licensed under a Creative Commons Attribution-NonCommercial 4.0 International License

Visit bernoff.com to sign up for daily writing tips with extra snark.

Source: withoutbullshit.com.

Embed Quotes and Links to
Enhance Your Credibility

Tables, graphics, headings, and lists break up text and make structure visible. But to bolster the authenticity of what you're writing, there are two more tools you can use: quotes and links.

Even within paragraphs, words in quotes stand out. But in documents, blog posts, and even emails, quoted material pulled out of the text draws your attention. I've used that technique throughout this book, including the quoted material from Augie Ray's blog at the start of this chapter.

And even though we know that our readers are now reading our material online, we sometimes forget about the power of links. Links let you reference *anything* online within any type of writing—an email, a web page, or a PDF document. Using links is second nature for bloggers, and it should be for you, too.

In most authoring systems, from Google Docs to Microsoft Word to the WordPress blog platform, you can insert a link just by highlighting a piece of text, pressing Ctrl+K (Command+K on a Mac), and pasting in the web address of a page that you've copied from the top of your browser. You can link to a news article, a blog post, a competitor's product page, a government report, a document on your intranet, a tweet, a Facebook post, a Google search, a video, or even a map. If it's on the web, you can link to it.

In web pages and blog posts, you can even embed tweets and videos. Go ahead. You'll enhance the meaning and make the page more interesting.

The Spirit of Writing

In chapters 3 through 11, I've shared everything I know about the principles of writing without bullshit. I hope you've seen how it all fits together. Do what I've said here, and you'll end up with writing that's tight, clear, direct, interesting, and easy to skim and navigate.

But as Morpheus told Neo in *The Matrix*, "There's a difference between knowing the path and walking the path." That's why we're not done. I've tried to help you see, not just why it's better to write this way, but why you didn't write this way in the first place. To get to the next stage—to write this way consistently—you must go further. You must change not just what you write, but how you write it.

Part Three

Change How You Write

12

Be Paranoid Early

So far in this book, I've concentrated on *what* you write. Now you've got a bunch of new habits to get into as you type anything, whether it's an email or a blog post. Follow those rules, and people will start seeing you differently.

Those rules are sufficient for tasks where the first draft plus a little polish is the final draft, but not for a big project.

Let's walk through your process for writing projects. You've got a big report due four weeks from now. It could be a white paper for your customers, an internal document to show your management team the health of your department, or a research paper that your company will use for planning. What's important is that we're talking about a piece of writing thousands of words long with lots of effort behind it.

For many writers, what comes next is less than ideal, a process that I call the three *P*s:

- **Procrastinate.** You can't start writing yet—you need to interview a few people, pull some data, and sit down and do some web research. Since you can't get started and the deadline is four weeks off, you do other pressing things on your schedule—things that have nothing to do with this project.

For a four-week project, the Procrastinate stage typically lasts about two weeks.

- **Panic.** Every writing project has this stage. It's when you realize that the amount of time left is *barely* enough for you to get the writing done. You leverage the urgency to complete the interviews that you need, run the data, and start finding some of what you'll need on the web. You start to write, recognize that something is missing, and then, blood pressure rising, hound whoever is supposed to help get it for you. You're writing, but with lots of interruptions to get the missing pieces in place. The end result comes together a few days before the deadline. If you have a few minutes to spare, you take a pass through the whole thing and smooth off a few of the rough edges, places where the structure is wonky, the language is inconsistent, or the facts are wrong.

- **Pray.** There's always somebody who has to approve it before you're done: your boss, the finance guy, the copy editor. So you send them the complete (but not finished) draft to review and tell them to turn it around in a day and a half. Hey, you're the writer—in a four-week process, you should get three and a half weeks, and those annoying reviewers can make do with a day or two. Concurrently with their reviews, you're fixing flaws you've already noticed, and as a result, lots of the review comments come back pointing out errors you just fixed or requesting changes in sentences you've deleted. You hope against hope that nobody finds something that will blow the whole thing up—and if they do, you find yourself arguing that it's better to live with the flaws than start over again. You put it all together and turn it in right on the deadline. Then you go home; have a scotch, a glass of wine, or a toke, depending on your preferred stress-relief method; and vow never to go through a process like that again.

Is it any wonder this process generates bullshit? Maybe things are this bad where you work, and maybe they're a little better. But unless you've got a disciplined writing process, you're not going to have enough time to get the structure, the tone, the theme, the language, and the title all right by the deadline. And there is *always* a deadline.

There must be a better way. And there is.

The Disciplined Process for Writing Without Bullshit

The key to writing an effective document in a business setting is to know what you're trying to accomplish at each stage and to put in equal effort at each stage, not to do everything at the end. When you know what you're working on at each moment, your results will improve steadily.

So let's revisit the three stages again, this time with a clearer understanding of what you're aiming for at each stage. For each, I include a slogan to help you dig in productively.

Stage 1: Prepare ("Be Paranoid Early")

Any piker can be paranoid when up against a deadline, where any little thing could destroy weeks of work.

It takes a professional to be paranoid at the start of the writing process. Being paranoid early means not just worrying about what might go wrong but also acting to prevent it. While late paranoia generates anxiety, early paranoia is productive.

Here's what to worry about and act on:

- **Do you have a clear audience and objectives?** Nail them down.
- **Do you have enough content?** (Answer: always no.) Develop a research plan and execute it. Find the holes and fill them.
- **Have you taken the most creative approach?** Stimulate ideas and marshal them systematically.
- **What is your structure?** Your objective is to create a "fat outline"—a description of what's going to be in the final piece and in what order.

Here's what you shouldn't be doing at this stage: writing. Writing without a plan or fuel is fruitless. Write up ideas, collect information, and reconsider titles—don't write the document.

I explain how to do all this in detail in the chapters that follow. Chapter 13 tells you how to lock down readers and objectives. Chapter 14 explains strategies for doing research and creating fat outlines. And chapter 15 is about getting in touch with your muse: creativity.

Stage 2: Draft ("Find Your Flow")

Writing takes concentration. By completing your research and planning ahead of time, you put yourself in a position to write well.

Your objective in this stage is to complete a draft. A complete draft is not a finished product—it is a complete piece of writing with flaws.

In a four-week process, writing the first draft should take about three days.

I explain how to maximize the value of a draft in chapter 15.

Stage 3: Revise ("Manage Reviews Effectively")

Drafting is not an end goal. It is simply the step that allows you to get to the Revise stage.

Revising is not a monolithic process either. Depending on how important your draft is, you'll need different levels of edits, each of which will get you closer to your goal: a bullshit-free finished document.

There is danger here. Editing and collaboration can make your document better; they can also ruin your clarity of purpose, make your writing inconsistent, and destroy the unity of what you have created. That's why the best writers maintain control of what they write throughout the process, responding to feedback with their own creativity. That's how you keep the bullshit out.

I explain how to collaborate effectively in chapter 17 and how to leverage edits in chapter 18. Chapter 19 tells you how best to be an effective editor.

I summarize the priorities for all these stages in figure 9.

How to Think About Process

If you look carefully at the stages I've described, you'll notice something surprising. The first draft is not where most of

FIGURE 9. What to do at each stage of the writing process.

Stage	Prepare	Draft	Revise
Slogan	Be paranoid early	Find your flow	Manage reviews effectively
What to do	Plan and do research	Find the right environment and write	Manage reviews and edits by stages
What to deliver	Research plan and fat outline	Complete draft	Polished final draft
What to worry about	Have I assembled everything I need?	Am I able to write a complete draft?	Have I prepared my reviewers properly?

the time and effort goes. Preparation and revising take more effort.

It's like running a marathon. The race takes two or three hours. But it takes months to prepare, and if running is your career, more months to analyze how you did and to improve. A marathon is a big effort, but it's not the only effort—a lot goes on before and after to make it successful.

The writing advice we concentrated on in the previous chapters comes into play, not just in the Draft stage but in every stage. You'll need to work hard to get the pieces you'll need—like numbers and graphics—in the Prepare stage. And you'll also need to work diligently to fend off the bullshit that inevitably creeps in during the Revise stage.

Lastly, a word about front-loading. As I described in chapter 5, titles, subtitles, first sentences, and summaries are crucial. You should be working on these *at every stage*. You should create a title up front, before you begin, and revisit it during the fat outline. You should include the executive summary in every draft. By the time you get to the end of the process, you'll have written two to four drafts, but you might have revised the title and summary ten times. That's worth the effort (and since they're short, it's not that much effort). Sometimes great titles come to mind immediately, but more often, they emerge from the process, and you must be open to them.

None of this matters if you're uncertain of your audience and objectives. I describe the systematic process for determining those key elements in the next chapter.

13

Think First

Business writing exists for one purpose: to create a change in the reader. If the reader is no different after reading, then you have wasted the reader's time and violated the Iron Imperative.

What sort of change do you want to make? That's a complex question. Before you start writing, you must think clearly about the elements of the change you are hoping to make.

ROAM: The Four Questions to Ask at the Start of Every Project

I use the acronym ROAM to help you keep track of the change you want to make in your readers. ROAM reflects the four elements of that change: Readers, Objective, Action, and iMpression. (As an acronym, ROAI would be more accurate but harder to remember.) As I describe in what follows, to determine those four elements at the start of a writing project, you must answer a question for each one (see figure 10).

FIGURE 10. ROAM: The four questions to ask before writing.

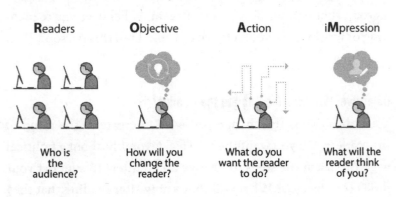

Readers	**O**bjective	**A**ction	i**M**pression
Who is the audience?	How will you change the reader?	What do you want the reader to do?	What will the reader think of you?

Readers: Who Is the Audience?

Before writing anything, visualize your readers. When you write "you," whom are you thinking of? Different audiences require different tone and different content. For example, if you write upward (to your boss, to senior managers), you'll typically write more briefly, while if you write downward (to your staff, to students) you can include more detail. A blog post for cattle ranchers will read far differently from a blog post for interactive marketers. If you don't know your readers, how can you write anything?

Barak Kassar, owner of a successful marketing agency in San Francisco, explains that when you are writing, a clear and specific conception of the audience is crucial. "I really try to literally imagine an actual living breathing person. What is that person like and what is going to make them tick?" he asks. "Because my style doesn't always align with that person, I try to get past writing for my own amusement or edification."

Here's how you can make that specific: Put a picture of a typical audience person in front of your computer when you write.

Put your favorite client there, or the CEO of the company, or a group shot of your development team. Whenever you're planning or writing, ask yourself, what would I tell this person? Then write that.

Objective: How Will You Change the Reader?

Your objective is the change you wish to create in the mind of the readers. Do you want them to feel favorably about a political party? to learn the steps to change an oil filter? to support your project? to feel joy? What will they know after reading that they did not know before?

Each element of your writing should guide the reader toward the objective. Cut anything that doesn't serve the objective. If you don't know your objective, how will you know what to include and what to leave out?

Action: What Do You Want the Reader to Do?

Once your readers are done reading, what will they do next? Objective and action are related, but not identical. The objective describes the change that you want to create in the reader, while the action is what the reader actually does: voting for the candidate, changing the oil filter, budgeting for the project, sharing the joyful writing with others. Among the writers in the WOBS Writing Survey who worked on writing projects, 72% said that their readers take action based on what they write.

Compared to objectives, actions are easier to spot and to measure. If you don't know the action you seek, how will you know if you succeeded? And if you don't expect your reader to do anything in particular after reading what you've written, why write it at all? Writing that does not create action is a waste. And writers who are wasting effort—their own or their readers'—don't keep their jobs for long.

iMpression: What Will the Reader Think of You?

Everything you write reflects on you, its author.

Objectives and actions may be fleeting, but impressions last. The impression is the metamessage. The readers' impression determines the future of your mutual relationship. Do you want readers to think of you as smart? trustworthy? witty? If you don't know the impression you hope to create, how will you know what style to write in?

As I promise in the subtitle of this book, you can boost your career by saying what you mean. In my survey, 67% of business writers agreed that they had impressed people through their writing. The iMpression element of ROAM is how writing boosts your career.

Put It Together in a Target Sentence

Once you've completed the ROAM analysis, you can write a single "target sentence" summarizing it. The sentence looks like this:

> After reading this piece, [readers] will realize [objective], so they will [desired action] and think of me/us as [desired impression].

Keep this sentence close by as you're writing. Test your work against it. Then you'll know if you're hitting the target.

The ROAM Analysis of Content Marketing

ROAM is very handy. As you'll see, I use it in the last five chapters of this book to analyze how to write various kinds of emails, social media posts, marketing materials, and reports. Starting with a ROAM analysis keeps your writing activities focused on what matters and channels your writing and editing toward a worthwhile goal.

Whether you're writing an email, a tweet, or a white paper, when you have that moment where you say "What am I doing here?" deploy ROAM. It will tell you what to do—and what not to.

Let's apply it to one of the hottest trends in writing and marketing right now: content marketing.

Content marketing means using blog posts and other helpful content to attract attention to your website and offerings. Hub-Spot, a company that makes tools for small- and medium-sized businesses, has mastered content marketing. It hosts a collection of useful blogs that attract folks in these businesses to the HubSpot website, where they can sign up to hear more about the company's products.

On December 22, 2015, HubSpot content marketer Lindsay Kolowich wrote a blog post called "12 Handy Tips for Running Better Remote Meetings." It begins like this:

> Whether you're meeting with colleagues who are working from home that day, or with clients located half a world away, running a productive and effective remote meeting can be a challenge.

When you're face-to-face with people, it can feel much easier to communicate efficiently and gauge how they're feeling and reacting to different ideas.

But when you're meeting virtually, it can seem like some attendees sort of . . . disappear into the abyss. [The post continues with (of course) 12 handy tips.]

Here's the ROAM checklist for her blog post:

- **Readers: workers in midmarket companies.** HubSpot focuses on companies with up to 900 employees. This post, naturally, is for workers in those businesses with colleagues who are located in other offices, who travel, or who work from home.
- **Objective: teach people about remote meeting tools.** Also, enable them to master the psychology of remote meetings.
- **Action: run remote meetings better.** Use the checklist in the blog post to have fewer screw-ups and better results after the meeting.
- **iMpression: HubSpot is helpful.** Leave readers feeling that HubSpot is a great partner that understands the needs of businesses like theirs.

Having completed this ROAM analysis, Kolowich might have written this target sentence:

After reading this blog post, workers in midmarket businesses will recognize that they need better tools and policies to make remote meetings productive, so they will run those meetings more effectively, and think of HubSpot as a helpful company.

In the ROAM analysis, notice the differences among the objective, action, and impression. The objective is to teach something. The desired action is to use the knowledge. And the desired impression is to work with HubSpot—which has nothing to do with remote meetings, but everything to do with being helpful.

Revise ROAM as Your Projects Move Forward

I've told you to do a ROAM analysis at the start of each writing project. But writing projects have a tendency to shift, going off course as management priorities, deadlines, reviews, and cool stuff that came to you as you were writing influence a project.

So double-check your ROAM checklist at the start of the Draft stage, and again at the start of the Revise stage. You might find yourself adjusting your objectives, the impression you're creating, or even your audience based on what you've learned. Your writing will be a lot better if you explicitly acknowledge that before you begin a draft.

14

Plan Purposefully

For six years, I wrote books while working in a research company. Everyone knew what I was working on, so they'd see me in the hall and ask, "How's the writing going?"

It always set my teeth on edge because if I answered truthfully, I'd have to say, "I haven't written anything!" I was working on the book. I just wasn't writing anything that would go into it. Yet.

If you're working on a project that's going to take more than a week, you probably have the same problem. You can't write anything yet because you don't have the raw material. But don't fall victim to the impulse to procrastinate. Here's how to make progress when you can't write: Write a title and opening, build a research plan, and create a fat outline.

Write a Title and Opening for Your Imagined Document

By this time, you've performed your ROAM analysis, so you know the readers, objective, action, and impression you have in mind. Pin the target sentence up in front of your computer where you can see it, or attach it to your monitor on a sticky note.

Now open a document, a blog post, or whatever you're writing, using whatever tool you'll be using to write it.

Now write your title at the top of the page.

"How am I supposed to do that?" you're thinking. "I don't know anything about what I'm going to write."

Do it anyway. You're about to have one of those naked-in-front-of-the-class moments. Imagine that you have to give a talk on this piece of writing 60 minutes from now. You certainly know *something*. And for certain, you know your audience, your objective, and the action you want readers to take.

So type "How to Create a Social Application for Life Sciences Without Getting Fired" (which was the actual title of a report I wrote). Or "The Three Reasons We Must Invest in a New Order Process." Or "Everything New Employees Need to Know at This Company." It's not the real, final title, so feel free to get a little silly.

Now start writing. Write the first paragraph of your document. Since you're completely unencumbered by research, write whatever you want. Just imagine that you're sitting across from a member of your future readership at a bar and tell them what you're going to tell them. Don't worry if it sucks; this isn't even the first draft, yet. For my life sciences report, I might have written something like this:

All marketers recognize the value of social media—tools like Facebook, Twitter, and blogs. Of course, with the marketing rules that the FDA puts in place, if you do it wrong, you could get a $250 million fine. That's scary, I know. But if you read what I've written here, you'll know what's worked for many life sciences companies—and how the marketers who created these applications managed to succeed, and to keep their jobs.

Now I'll explain *why* I just put you through this exercise. First off, the title is more important than anything else you'll be writing; now you'll be able to revise it as you learn more about your topic. Openings are crucial, too. As you do your research, you'll have this opening in your head, and you'll be thinking of ways to improve it.

You also just inoculated yourself against writer's block. When the time comes to write, you won't have to worry about getting started because you already did.

Save your work—call it "Life sciences social report draft 1" or whatever it would be if you were actually writing. Go get up and get a cup of coffee (unless you're on an airplane). And when your coworker walks up and says, "How's the writing going?" you can say, "Well, I'm off to a good start."

Create and Execute a Research Plan

You have no content. You might have some ideas, but you need more. You need research. Don't start searching, calling, and emailing just yet. You need a plan.

Every document requires web research. Build time into your schedule for searching and reading online content. What you need is on the web, on your corporate intranet, or in your company's information systems. Use these sources to get the numbers, quotes, examples, and proof points that will make your piece more believable. Keep a list of bookmarks or URLs so you can find content again when you need it. While it's not required, a note-taking system with tags, such as Evernote or Microsoft OneNote, helps organize this task.

If you're going to conduct interviews, internal or external, you'll want to track them carefully as well. Here's how to do that:

Open up a spreadsheet. Google Sheets is ideal for this. It's right in your browser, where you're going to do your web research anyway, and it allows you to easily collaborate with anybody else who's going to be researching alongside you. (Go ahead and use Microsoft Excel for this if you like it better, but if you're working with coauthors or assistants, recognize that Google Sheets is better designed for collaboration.) If you're a database whiz, you can track contacts in a database like salesforce.com, but for most mortals a spreadsheet is sufficient.

I've seen lots of elaborate tracking spreadsheets, but yours can be as simple as you want. You just need columns for the type of research (external interview, coworker interview, web research), the contact's name, the contact information (email, phone), the most recent date of contact, status (emailed, recontacted, setting up interview, scheduled, completed), and notes. I also include a "Priority" column, in which I put "1" for must-have interviews to "5" for nice-to-haves. (See figure 11.)

This will sound excessively fussy, but I have one more piece of advice. *Track each research contact on a separate row.* Do not include empty rows or rows with headings. Why? Because then you can sort and resort the spreadsheet by priority, status, or any other way you want.

Work on this for at least a few days, adding to and changing it as you and your colleagues come up with research ideas. And now when somebody asks, "How's the writing going?" you can

FIGURE 11. A research-tracking spreadsheet.

	A	B	C	D	E	F	G
1	Research	Priority	Company	Last	First	Status	Date of last contact
2	Case Study	1	Dell	Pearson	Bob	Completed	3/1/2008
3	Case Study	1	TiVo	Poniatowski	Bob	Completed	4/1/2008
4	Vendor	1	Digg	Adelson	Jay	Completed	3/15/2008
5	Case Study	1	Del Monte	Amoroso	Gala	Completed	4/1/2008
6	Case Study	1	Procter & Gamble	Arnold	Bob	Scheduled	4/12/2008
7	Case Study	2	Lego	Askildson	Tormod	Completed	3/19/2008
8	Case Study	2	AACS	Ayers	Michael B.	Completed	3/19/2008
9	Case Study	2	Intuit	Ballabio	Stephanie	Completed	4/12/2008
10	Case Study	2	Intel	Bancroft	Josh	Setting up	4/12/2008
11	Case Study	2	Best Buy	Bendt	Steven	Scheduled	3/1/2008
12	Case Study	2	salesforce.com	Benioff	Mark	Contacted	4/1/2008
13	Case Study	2	Ernst & Young	Black	Dan	Setting up interview	3/15/2008
14	Expert	2	Market Evolution	Briggs	Rex	Setting up interview	4/1/2008
15	Case Study	2	Emerson Process	Cahill	Jim	Scheduled	4/12/2008
16	Vendor	2	Visible Technologies	Cahill	Blake	Scheduled	3/19/2008
17	Vendor	2	BzzAgent	Chernov	Joe	Setting up interview	3/19/2008
18	Case Study	2	Sony	Clancy	Rick	Scheduled	3/1/2008
19	Case Study	2	eBags	Cobb	Peter	Scheduled	4/1/2008
20	User	2	Joe Comeau	Comeau	Joe	Setting up interview	3/15/2008

answer, truthfully, "We're making a lot of progress on the research."

Now it's time to contact people. Here are some tips I've learned from decades of research:

- **Send individual emails, not mass emails.** People ignore mass emails and are far less likely to get back to you. Consider it the corollary to the Iron Imperative: You must treat the interviewee's time as more valuable than your own. Craft a separate email for each person. Be careful when copying and pasting content; don't insult somebody by sending an email with somebody else's information in it. I've got more advice on crafting an email that gets a callback in chapter 21.
- **Use Facebook, Twitter, or LinkedIn messages as alternate contact channels.** You can often get people to respond more quickly in these channels than in email.

- **Have interview questions ready ahead of time.** This is another way to treat the interview subject's time as valuable. Start with easy questions, ask follow-ups, and then, with trust established, get into the challenging and detailed questions. Don't leave anything out; follow-up calls are tough to schedule and annoying to the interviewee.
- **Keep good records to make follow-up and fact-checking easier.** And if you've promised an interviewee a copy of the finished document, you'll have that contact list up-to-date in your spreadsheet.

Make a Fat Outline

Before you start drafting, you need a plan for your document. You probably learned to make an outline somewhere in school. But what you learned is useless for planning to write.

The purpose of an outline is to help you and the people you're working with—your boss, your clients, your editor—understand what you're going to write. And, it should also force *you*, the writer, to think clearly about content.

Traditional outlines suck for this.

For example, here's an outline of the first part of this book:

Part One: Change Your Perspective
Chapter 1: Transcend Bullshit
The Iron Imperative
Measuring Meaning
One Woman's Path to Success

Could This Be You?

Join Me on a Journey of Clarity and Candor

Chapter 2: Seize Your Opportunity

We Spend All Day Reading on Screens

No One Edits What We Read

We Learned to Write the Wrong Way

Is this the outline of a good book? No one could possibly know. It's like looking at the skeleton of a potential blind date and trying to figure out if you think they're attractive. You need some meat on the bones.

You need a fat outline. A fat outline is more like a treatment for a movie—it includes pieces of the actual content. It flips between writing that will potentially be in the final piece, descriptions of potential content, and promises of future content. It's harder to write than a traditional outline because you have to think about it, but that's why it's useful.

When writing a fat outline, ignore grammar and other traditional writing (and outlining) rules because you're just showing how you'll organize the content. If you show it to editors or collaborators, they can critique the organization but they shouldn't edit the words. For example, here's a fat outline for the first part of this book.

Part One: Change Your Perspective

This part analyzes the trends that generate bullshit, as a preliminary to the actual writing advice.

Chapter 1: Transcend Bullshit

The tide of bullshit is rising. Your inbox is full of . . . a cri de coeur to tap into the reader's outrage. Promise that if you read the book and learn to write boldly you'll stand out. I will give you the courage to say what you mean.

Iron Imperative Definition: You must treat the reader's time as more valuable than your own. Explain why people tend not to do this. Adopt the Iron Imperative or put the book down.

Measuring meaning. Define bullshit. Define the "meaning ratio": meaningful words out of total words. Calculate for Inovalon description; show alternative.

One woman's path to success: Tell Diane Hessan's story. Entrepreneur who succeeded with candor and boldness. Include sample of her email.

Could this be you? More stories. Need three more quick case studies, one paragraph each.

Join me on a journey of clarity and candor. Lay out the sections and chapters in the rest of the book.

Chapter 2: Seize Your Opportunity
Quotes from William Zinsser and Harry Frankfurt for historical perspective. Then lay out three reasons we're drowning in clutter.

We spend all day reading on screens. Smartphone owners spend 3.3 hours per day on their screens (salesforce.com), half of phone users use them in bathroom (Forrester), those under 70 more likely to read media online than in print (Forrester). More stats to come.

Now there's some meat on the bones. You know what to research, and you know what's missing. You know where to plug in the research. And if you work with an editor, they can see what you're planning and have a meaningful conversation. Editors who approve traditional outlines have, frankly, no idea what they're getting. Editors who read your fat outline can tell you where you may be going wrong and where they've got suggestions for research that can help.

Open up the document that you created earlier with the title and first paragraph. Type your fat outline there. If you find the fat outline difficult to write, *figure out why*. It's not because you don't know which words to use—because the fat outline is just a rough description, and the words don't matter. Are you unsure of your audience? Are you unclear about what you ought to research? Are you not sure what order to put things in or what belongs together? Fling your thoughts into that outline draft, massage them around, add that funny turn of phrase you thought of or the stats you know are out there and you're going to track down. Now you're getting somewhere—even though you're still planning and not yet actually writing.

Keep Revising as You Work

Everything I've described in this chapter is fluid. Think about your title idea every few days, and revise your title and opening. Keep your research tracking spreadsheet up-to-date, and concentrate on those key interviews that haven't come in yet or those statistics you need to track down. Revise the fat outline once or twice before you begin writing, adding in the bits and pieces and insights you've acquired along the way.

Now all you need to do is unleash your creativity—I'll explain how in the next chapter—and you'll be ready to begin writing.

15

Unleash Creativity

Creativity is what makes good writing stand out. It's what makes the reader sit up and take notice, because they're reading something unexpected.

Somehow, creativity got associated with fiction. But anyone who reads the likes of Malcolm Gladwell or Mary Roach knows that fascinating nonfiction is every bit as creative as fiction.

What about business writing? Should your reports be creative? Should your blog posts and press releases be fascinating?

Maybe if they were, people would read them and remember them.

But what should you do if you are not creative?

Rethink who you are.

How to Be Creative

When I started as an analyst at Forrester Research in the '90s, I had come from a background of mathematics and software development. I had run the production department for a publishing company. I thought of myself as a problem solver who was pretty good at putting words together.

The analyst job required me to research and then write reports. Of my first four reports, three were problematic: weak research, mundane ideas, missed deadlines.

At the end of the year, the company held a meeting of all the staff. About a hundred people were crammed into two connected conference rooms. The big bosses began to hand out awards for the people who most exemplified company values like quality and service. I was sad because I admired these people greatly and knew that I was failing to live up to the potential they saw in me. I wondered when they would fire me.

As I stewed in my self-pitying reverie, somebody slapped me on the shoulder. They had just announced me as the winner of the annual Forrester Research Creativity Award. I was so shocked, I could not speak. (That's pretty rare.)

The idea that I was creative was new to me. But I was open to it. It sure beat getting fired.

At that moment, I decided, "What the heck, if they think I'm creative, then I'll damn well embrace it." So I determined to be as creative as I could be.

It is in my nature to look for a strange, warped way to put a spin on anything people say, write, or do. (It comes from a legacy of constant pun making.) Whatever someone says, I flip it. If they are talking about American business, I think of how it would be different in Japan. I imagine a contrary world in which Bill O'Reilly is a flaming liberal and Bill Maher is an archconservative, or where the accountants are libertines and the artists wear green eyeshades. Once you twist the perspective, you see the absurdity.

Forrester built its reputation on finding unconventional and novel insights into how markets worked. So I applied my talents to finding new perspectives on business: that the TV schedule was irrelevant, that the Internet was splintering into pieces, that business transactions would focus on tiny instants of time.

I did pretty well with that. I justified their judgment that I was creative.

Now I'm going to do for you what Forrester's management did for me. As of this moment, I am giving you the creativity award. You are the most creative marketing copywriter, customer service representative, small-business salesperson, or entrepreneur. You picked up a book called *Writing Without Bullshit*, didn't you? There must be a rebellious streak in you. Let it out.

Your creativity will now generate the startling, fascinating ideas you need to make your writing stand out.

The pressure is on, but I won't leave you on your own. Here are some counterintuitive tips on unleashing your creativity:

- **Embrace your frustration.** If you're having a problem, other people are, too. Their problem may be your next opportunity. Scott Cook, founder of Intuit, once explained to me how small-business owners would call the support line for its Quicken product and complain about the product. It drove the support staff crazy, since they had to explain over and over that they had designed Quicken for individuals, not businesses. Finally, Cook realized the problem was an opportunity. Quicken created a small-business product called QuickBooks, which grew into a $500 million revenue stream.
- **Turn your world upside down.** If you've always sold products, what would happen if your company sold services instead? What customers have you never been able to reach—

and what not-yet-tried strategy would reach them if that was the only way to save your company? If all your customers could leave tomorrow, how would you win them back? Imagine a world completely different from the one you live in. What new ideas would enable you to succeed in that world?

- **Get a new perspective.** Talk to your sister. Talk to your architect. Call up your old friend who works in the government of the state of New Hampshire. If you're 55, talk to somebody who's 25 (and vice versa). Imagine, just for a moment, that the person you're listening to has some deep insight that you are missing. You may see things through their eyes, even if they don't see the same things themselves.
- **Stop working for a minute.** You're a lot less likely to see that new idea when you're going all out at 300 miles per hour. Take a day off. Take an hour off. Do that evening commute with the radio off and the smartphone in your purse. Just think. Muse. It'll come to you.

How to Develop Ideas

Creative thinking generates new ideas. Some of them suck. Others need time to mature. They don't develop themselves. You need to work at it.

I spent so much time working on ideas at Forrester—my own and those of other people—that the management there eventually gave me the title "Senior Vice President, Idea Development." It was more than just words on a business card. I helped develop ideas every day.

Perversely, the most important element of idea development

is a set of deadlines. Unless there is pressure to produce something by a given date, you're unlikely to conceive something and finish it. To meet deadlines, you need a cauldron of possible content simmering. But that's not enough.

The other key element is idea fuel. Ideas come from everywhere if you are in the right state of mind. For example, I am constantly on the lookout for ideas about good writing, bad writing, writing methods, teaching of writing, sources of bullshit, effects of bullshit, effects of saying what you actually mean, and related topics. My mind relates anything I watch, read, hear, or discuss to these topics. This includes not only the usual web research, but also conversations with others (in person or on social media), articles I read, and the whole of my current and past experience.

You should do the same thing, but on whatever topic you are interested in. Treat every conversation, every article you read, and every interaction—including with retail salespeople and your kids—as fuel.

The result of all this activity will be unformed concepts, most of which are not yet actual ideas. Keep track of them somewhere. (I've already mentioned Evernote as a research tool, but it's also a good app for collecting and organizing ideas in one notebook accessible on any smartphone, tablet, or computer.)

Concepts are not yet ideas, but if you develop them, they can be. Ideas evolve. What does it take to turn a concept into an idea? You have to connect it with other concepts and content, and your experience. Most of all, it needs a "hook"—that is, a quick and intriguing way of describing what you mean.

Once you've got an idea with a hook, you're onto something, but you're not nearly done. Pull together content you find online, in your notes, or from interviews and conversations. Then assemble and shape those bits of content into prose and use it in whatever you're writing.

Most people don't think about this process in any formal way (or they may be superstitious, believing that it loses its magic when you think about it). But you should be developing ideas mentally all the time, in parallel with everything else you do. Even as you are researching, solving problems, or working, you should be semiconsciously turning over bits and pieces of ideas and trying to fit them into a structure. Then when you sit down to write, all that activity, together, generates something worth reading.

Idea development turns creativity into written pieces you can use. Start early, and give concepts time to gestate. Your writing will be better when you're done.

16
Find Flow

In 1961, Kurt Vonnegut Jr. published the short story "Harrison Bergeron." It's a masterpiece of ironist thinking in 2,200 words. It begins like this: "The year was 2081, and everybody was finally equal."

The reason people are equal in 2081 is that the government has taken the necessary steps to make them equal. If you have any outstanding qualities, then Diana Moon Glampers, the government's Handicapper General, will ensure that you cannot use them.

If you are graceful, you must wear weights on your ankles. If you are beautiful, you must wear a mask. And if you are more intelligent . . . well, here's how Vonnegut explains it through the experience of two characters, George and his wife, Hazel:

George, while his intelligence was way above normal, had a little mental handicap radio in his ear. He was required by law to wear it at all times. It was tuned to a government transmitter. Every twenty seconds or so, the transmitter would send out some sharp noise to keep people like George from taking unfair advantage of their brains.

George and Hazel were watching television. There were tears

on Hazel's cheeks, but she'd forgotten for the moment what they were about.

On the television screen were ballerinas.

A buzzer sounded in George's head. His thoughts fled in panic, like bandits from a burglar alarm.

Vonnegut never anticipated that there would be no need for the mental handicap radio. In the 50-plus years since he wrote this story, we've embraced distraction. Our ears are plugged with headphones. We work in noisy open offices rife with interruptions. We've got email, Facebook, and smartphones to divert us all day long.

You cannot write well if you cannot concentrate for more than 20 seconds at a time. You've handicapped yourself far more effectively than Diana Moon Glampers ever could.

Here's why and how to maintain your concentration.

The Psychology of Flow

The brilliant psychologist Mihaly Csikszentmihalyi describes the experience of "flow"—of being productive and in the moment, making rapid progress on work that matches well to your skills. Flow happens when you have a task to complete, one that's difficult but not impossible. To achieve flow, you must be able to make steady progress, solving problems as you go along. To a writer, flow feels great. But more importantly, flow creates great writing.

As Susan K. Perry put it in her book *Writing in Flow,* "You know you've been in flow when time seems to have disappeared.

When you're in flow, you become so deeply immersed in your writing, or whatever activity you're doing, that you forget yourself and your surroundings."

You're not going to create fluid, fascinating, persuasive prose writing a sentence at a time, punctuated by checking email and Facebook, returning phone calls, and getting coffee. Your piece will read a lot better if you write it all at once or in large chunks such as sections or chapters.

Like any great intellectual accomplishment, attaining flow requires the right preparation, the right environment, and a knowledge of how your brain works.

In the last few chapters, I've talked about the importance of preparation—thinking through audience and objectives, doing research ahead of time, writing openings, making fat outlines, and priming yourself to be creative. This is not just a matter of hitting deadlines. While you are preparing, your mind is wrestling with the challenge of what you're writing. That process, much of which is unconscious, is a necessary prerequisite.

If you do this work ahead of time, then when you're ready to write, you will have removed the obstacles that would otherwise get in your way. You will have assembled the ideas, facts, quotes, organization, and knowledge you need to begin writing. Unless you do this first, you'll never attain flow.

How to Concentrate

Everything in your workspace is conspiring against you. Your computer, your smartphone, your colleagues—they're all potential distractions and interruptions. As my former Forrester

Research colleague, the author James McQuivey, explains, "To write, I have to separate myself from the routine distractions of life."

I love the moment of sitting and creating. You may hate it. But we both need uninterrupted concentration to create writing that flows. This demands two things: time and space.

First, time. Get yourself at least 90 minutes when you won't be interrupted. If your workday is full of meetings, this might be at night or on the weekend. If that's not workable for you, block off time during your day when you won't be interrupted (with a 15-minute buffer before and after). Match your natural daily cycle. Learn whether you're more productive at 5:30 a.m., late in the morning, in the afternoon, in the evening, or late at night.

Next, space. You need a writing place where coworkers won't interrupt you in person or on the phone. You might prefer to work at home or at an unoccupied desk. In some workplaces, putting on headphones tells your coworkers you can't be interrupted. Some people do their best work on airplanes; the coauthor on one of my books did most of his writing in a coffee shop.

I like silence. Some people like to blast music. I like plants around me. You might like bare walls. Surround yourself with the things that make you productive but don't distract you.

Your brain needs fuel. Your blood sugar level matters. Ideally, you'll have eaten a meal a few hours before. Brains that are low on blood sugar don't concentrate well. And consuming sugar or caffeine before writing amps up your brain but doesn't put you into a flow state—you're looking for steady concentration, not jittery hyperawareness.

Next, content. Open up the tools you use to collect notes, interviews, and other content. Open up the fat outline and put it where you can see it and refer to it. Writing creates questions: What example supports this? What's the productivity statistic? What analogy can I use to prove this point? By having the elements of your writing close at hand, you reduce the likelihood that you'll have to stop and look something up or call somebody—activities that will interfere with your flow.

Lastly, purge the everyday distractions of social media and email. Turn your phone off. You're entering the sacred writing space. Don't let anything destroy that.

Now you can start writing.

Keep going until you get stuck. But when you get stuck, write yourself a note about what you need to fix (for example, "transition needed here") and then continue. Optimally, you'll write in 30- to 60-minute bursts with five or ten minutes in between. If you write in 10-minute bursts with 30 minutes in between, your writing will be choppy. You won't achieve flow.

What to Do If You Fail

Sometimes, flow is elusive. It just doesn't come together. You create crap, and you know it is crap even as you create it. Your structure doesn't match the content. Your writing is not convincing. You feel like a failure.

At this point, you need to remember how the mind solves problems.

Consider the experience of the Irish mathematician William Rowan Hamilton in 1843. Hamilton had seen how productive it was to extend the usual number line into two dimensions to create so-called complex numbers. He was attempting to extend the concept of numbers further, into additional dimensions. Each day, he worked on possibilities. Each day, he failed.

One day he took a stroll along the Royal Canal in Dublin with his wife. While walking across a bridge, Hamilton suddenly had a counterintuitive stroke of insight—as he described it, "An electric circuit seemed to close; and a spark flashed forth"—and the solution to the problem was in his mind. He immediately carved a simple set of equations into a stone at the side of the bridge. He dubbed the new numbers he had invented quaternions. Hamilton worked on and taught about quaternions for the rest of his life, and there is now a plaque commemorating his discovery on the bridge in Dublin.

Solving the problems of writing—of fitting concepts together— is not all that different from solving mathematical problems. It requires hard work, like the work that Hamilton did. Although you may think you have made no progress, your mind is turning over possibilities and ideas, and your own electrical circuit will close when it is ready.

When you fail, your brain does not give up, even if you think you have. To make progress from that point, you need relaxation that occupies your conscious mind, like Hamilton's stroll along the canal. Personally, I often find these solutions come to me while cycling, exercising, or lying in bed not sleeping.

Succeeding on a challenging problem requires four ingredients: hard work, failure, relaxation, and time. Unless you have all four, you won't get beyond the obstacle.

What does this mean for writing? It means that you must work hard *before* you begin writing, challenging yourself to find the right content and organization for that content. You must recognize that failure is a step on the way. And you must have the time to allow your mind to come up with new solutions while you do something else.

Writing seems linear, but creation is not. Your process must acknowledge that. And when you return to the keyboard, having solved the knotty problem in your head, you'll find flow far easier to attain.

Don't Screw It Up

You've created a draft, and you're happy with it.

Now you're going to show it to other people. And they're going to tell you it's wrong. Not only that, they'll have good points. You'll need to address them.

As you proceed into the Revise stage, you don't want to lose what you worked so hard to create.

The chapters that follow this one describe my advice on how to work collaboratively and how to revise. But here's a rule of thumb: Try not to add too much. Cut what doesn't work. Fix what's frayed and the transitions that don't work. Rearrange to improve structure. But preserve the fluid elements of what you created.

Flow is hard to get. Don't give up the fruits of flow too easily.

17

Collaborate Without Tears

The best thing about writing in a business setting is that there are so many people to help.

The problem with writing in a business setting is that there are so many people to meddle.

Here's what you need to know: It's your document. You're writing it, and your name is probably going to go on it. I've told you how to boost your career by writing without bullshit. Now I'm going to tell you how to write with other people, without losing the soul of what you write.

The first thing to understand is everybody's role in the process.

Roles in the Writing Process

Businesses have lots of people who help them: lawyers, accountants, consultants, and so on. As long as the people running the business recognize that these people are advisors, they're fine. If you let them take over, it's not your business anymore.

Similarly, if you're writing with reviewers and collaborators, there are a lot of people who are there to offer advice, content, or help. If you don't take advantage of them, you're missing out. But if you let them take over, it's not your writing anymore.

Let's get an understanding of who you might be working with as a writer, what they do, and where they fit into the writing process. Be aware that not every project includes all these roles.

Editors and Project Managers Work Throughout the Process

An editor makes writing better. If you can find someone intelligent and experienced to review your work from beginning to end, sign that person up. If somebody else assigns you an editor, that editor is probably experienced enough to help you a lot. Either way, you'll learn a lot if you listen to your editor.

Editors stand in for the reader. They tell you what they think the reader needs, or won't understand, in what you've written. If they've got any talent, they also suggest how to fix things.

Ideally, an editor starts with you during the preparation stage, helping to define your readers, your objectives, the action you want to generate, and the impression you want to make (remember ROAM?). Diligent editors will also review and comment on your research plan and fat outline. They review each draft and provide the appropriate level of feedback. And most importantly, they'll tell you when you're done.

A great editor also encourages you, tells you when you've gone too far, and points out where you could do better.

The next chapter explains the editing process in more detail. For now, just recognize that an experienced editor is your key writing partner.

The other job that some editors do is to manage the whole

writing process, interacting with your other reviewers and coordinating the feedback you get. But sometimes that's someone else's job: a project manager or traffic person who keeps track of everything, manages the flow of drafts and comments, and hammers on deadlines. Frankly, though, unless you're part of a big, mature writing team, you'll probably have to manage these reviews yourself.

Researchers and Contributors Help During the Research Phase

For big writing projects, you can't do it all yourself. That's where researchers and contributors come in.

Researchers do a lot of the legwork for you and can find the data, facts, and content you need to beef up a piece of writing. These are often bright entry-level staffers. Turn them loose with clear instructions on what you need, and they'll find great content for you. And because they don't think exactly like you, they're likely to find things you would never have tracked down. Researchers can also help with the time-consuming and tedious process of setting up and tracking interviews, as I described in chapter 14.

Depending on what you're writing, you may also get help from other specialized contributors. For example, as you develop content ideas, you'll have ideas for graphics—pull in a designer or illustrator to work with you just as you're starting your draft. If you've got to include specialized content—financial analysis, for example, or a technical discussion—you can get contributions from experts in those subjects. But leave time in your drafting process to rework their contributions to match the rest of what you're writing.

Advisory Reviewers Comment on Your Drafts

Your organization probably includes experts who can help you in many ways—with ideas, with structure, or with content knowledge, for example. Don't just sit there. Ask them for help.

I call these helpers "advisory reviewers," a term that refers to anyone who can help you make your writing better but does not have final approval.

To successfully manage feedback from these reviewers, fit them into your process based on their skills. If you know people who are good with ideas, get their help at the fat outline stage. Folks with specialized knowledge can help once there's a draft to work on. Those who are great with words can help when the draft is getting closer to finished. Don't wait until the end for all these reviews, or you'll get lots of great ideas that you can't fit into the finished product.

Make sure your editor—your primary reviewer—knows who you're working with. And be clear with reviewers about expectations. Tell these folks the specific kind of help you want from them. And let them know that while you expect to include their suggestions in the final draft, you and your editor will have to make the decisions about what goes in and what has to get left behind.

Gatekeeping Reviewers Get the Last Look

Gatekeepers are folks whose edits you're not allowed to ignore. For example, legal and regulatory reviews fall into this category. Sometimes your boss does, too.

People fear gatekeepers, but they are there for a reason: to keep you from screwing up. Sometimes you have to listen because they control the piece of the company you're contributing to.

Be bold here, not fearful. If you anticipate problems with gate-keepers, ask them to do reviews early in the process. This can help you to avoid getting derailed at the end by a request that mucks up your beautiful prose. And by showing them you respect their input, you can help get them on your side.

Your approach to obligatory reviews will, inevitably, depend on how much power they have. Your boss (and in some cases, your peers) may have the power not just to change what you've written but also to determine the future of your job. Does this mean you must do as the gatekeepers say? No. What it means is that you must take their concerns seriously and respond to them carefully. Reviewers of this type deserve a respectful note if you decide that you cannot or should not make the changes they request exactly as they request them. If your bosses are huge fans of jargon and passive voice, for example, give them a copy of this book and then have a thoughtful discussion about writing.

Regardless of who your gatekeepers are, here's what not to do: drop off a 12-page document and tell them at that moment that you need it back the next day. That's disrespectful and annoying, and the last thing you need is a pissed-off gatekeeper who can sink your project or make you work all night to fix it. Much better is to apprise the gatekeeper ahead of time on what will be coming and give them some time to review it.

Copy Editors and Fact-Checkers Keep You Safe at the End

When you think you're done with a document, you turn it over to the copy editor. The copy editor's job is to look for grammar and usage errors. But just as with any other reviewer, don't assume you must do everything the copy editor says—it's still your document.

This endpoint is also when you check facts and quotes. Most organizations can no longer afford separate fact-checkers, but if you have one, they'll check to make sure you're not lying about the population of Sri Lanka or what the senior senator from Missouri said. If you don't have a fact-checker, then get used to checking everything yourself before it gets published.

The Magic Words

I've summarized the types of contributors and reviewers in figure 12.

These folks all have one thing in common.

You're asking for their help. And they're responding with critiques and content.

This works a lot better if you're gracious—even if what you're asking for, criticism, is distressing for you. You need to stay on these people's good side. So remember the magic words:

"Thank you."

That goes a long way, especially when everyone is working toward a deadline.

Collaboration Tools

If you work with other people, you'll be a lot better off with technology that allows you all to share your work efficiently.

The old way of doing this was to store stuff on your hard drive and then email it to people you were working with. This is fraught with problems. Raise your hand if you've experienced the "damn, you edited the wrong version" problem. It happens all the time.

FIGURE 12. Roles of the potential contributors in writing projects.

Type of contributor	What they do	Ideal time to contribute
Primary author(s)	Plan, write, revise	Prepare, Draft, and Revise stages
Editor	Overall guidance; stand-in for the reader	Prepare, Draft, and Revise stages
Project manager	Keep project on track; enforce deadlines	Prepare, Draft, and Revise stages
Researcher	Track down facts and content	Prepare stage
Contributors	Add specific content (e.g., data analysis)	Prepare and Draft stages
Advisory reviewers	Review based on technical or other expertise	Revise stage: early drafts
Gatekeeping reviewers	Review and approve (e.g., legal review)	Revise stage: middle to late drafts
Fact-checkers	Verify facts and quotes	Revise stage: final draft
Copy editors	Check for correct grammar and usage	Revise stage: final draft

There are sophisticated trafficking systems that some organizations use to manage content, but they come with a lot of overhead. You don't need that. You just need the cloud.

Since I'm supposed to be a jargon fighter, let me explain what I mean by that.

Start with a shared folder. Google Drive or Dropbox works great for this. You can organize the content in that folder with source materials and drafts. This not only lets you collaborate with coworkers but also lets you access the bits and pieces from whatever device you want. Set things up properly and the folder will replicate to your hard drive and store all versions of what you're working on, so you've got a nice, safe automatic backup. "The hard drive crashed and ate my draft" is no excuse in the 21st century.

There are two basic ways to manage collaboration on a document: Microsoft Word or Google Docs.

If you're writing something that will eventually appear in print as well as online, use Microsoft Word because it supports more precise page-level formatting. Reviewers should make a copy of your Microsoft Word draft and mark it up with Word's reviewing tools, which reflect all revisions, additions, deletions, and comments.

Don't email files. Instead, share the file, the link to the Google Docs page, or the whole folder and tell the reviewers to edit that. This allows you to fix the inevitable few little problems you notice just *after* you tell the reviewers to have at it. They'll always be reviewing the latest version.

One more specific suggestion: adopt file-naming conventions to save you from collaboration chaos. My files have names like "WWB book 06 Passive v1.doc." (Translation: *Writing Without Bullshit*, chapter 6, Passive Voice, first draft.) The numbering allows you to sort the filenames easily and see what's there, what's updated, and what's missing. Remember that these files will also appear on someone else's hard drive or folder. They will spot your content a lot easier if it's not just called "marketing blog post" or "Chapter 5." The version number allows you to communicate clearly about what they're looking at. When they send it back, it should have the same name with something like "HH edits" tacked on, to indicate that HH has edited it.

In chapter 14, I showed how to use Google Sheets to track research interviews. They're also great for tracking elements such as chapters, chapter titles, who's working on which pieces, and deadlines. And, in contrast to the text, you'll *want* multiple people to be able to update these tracking sheets at the same time.

You'll want to share your notes with researchers and editors, too. You can do this with folders or with tools like Evernote.

Finally, get used to using Skype (or similar video communication tools, such as Google Hangouts). You can Skype with another person anywhere in the world when you both have a computer. You'll want to see your editor's face, even if they're in Singapore and you're in Mumbai, to see if they're actually upset or just being sarcastic. You'll both need to have access to the shared files. (Editorial meetings in which one person is in the back of a taxi don't work so well.)

Working with a Coauthor

Working with all those other people is relatively easy because you're still in charge of the writing. You just need to decide how to deal with their advice and contributions.

But what if you have a coauthor? Then two people are responsible, together, for one piece of content.

This can work great. But unless you resolve the responsibility and process issues up front, you're in for trouble. The communications overhead between you will more than double the amount of work you need to do. So here's how to work with a coauthor without killing yourself (or each other).

To start, recognize that this is an intense relationship. I've coauthored three books, and I found that it was the intellectual equivalent of getting married. It was that intimate, getting it right was just as rewarding, and getting it wrong was just as painful. Even if you're collaborating on something smaller than a book, if you care about it, then sharing it will be challenging.

Just as with your editor, start by agreeing on your readers, objectives, desired action, and hoped-for impression. Do the ROAM analysis together. Complete the target sentence:

> After reading what we have written, [group of people] will re-alize that [change in thinking], so they will [action they will take], and they'll start to think of us as [desired impression].

Once you've settled on the target sentence, pick a title. *Do not go forward without agreeing on a title.* Unless you agree on that up front, you'll end up fighting over it. Brainstorming the title together will also help you learn a lot more about what you're doing together.

Toss a fat outline back and forth until you're happy with it. That outline then becomes the heart of your planning. Divide up not just the pieces of content but also the tasks—writing, research, data analysis, graphics—so you each know what you are responsible for. For example, you'll write the first two parts, and your coauthor will edit; and then she'll write the ending part, and you'll edit. Or you'll do all the research, and she'll do all the writing.

Remember, if both of you do everything in duplicate, you'll drown in a lack of productivity. It's not necessary that one person be in charge, but it *is* necessary that each task has a leader responsible for that task (lead researcher, lead visionary, lead data analyst, person in charge of words, person who negotiates with publishers, and so on).

Agree on a schedule and deadline. Figure out whose name goes first (typically the more well-known person or the one who originated the idea).

One of you is a better writer. That person should establish the voice for the writing and do most of the wordcrafting. The other author should match that style. (If you both have the same voice, then you are actually one person with a schizoid complex.)

Determine a rigorous process for completing, reviewing, and finalizing pieces, including who does what in what order and when each draft or element is completed.

Break down what happens at the end, too. When it's time to roll the thing out, who will do the promotion? Who will deal with management?

And finally, I beg you, listen to this last piece of advice. *Do not have more than two authors.* With three authors, the overhead multiplies and politics emerge as two-against-one alliances form. I could show you the scars. Just don't do it.

Remember that your writing is your baby, but your coauthor is your friend. Sometimes the relationship requires you to give up on a passionately held idea to keep the project on track. And sometimes, it turns out, you're wrong, and your coauthor is right. You picked each other for a reason.

18
Embrace Edits

"I love criticism . . ."

. . . said no one, ever.

Early in my writing career, a wise writer told me that until I learned to embrace criticism, I would never get any better. He was right. But it's like a Zen koan: how can you learn to love hearing about your flaws? Writers are proud. Criticism *hurts*.

Well, it turns out there's a trick to it.

The first part of the trick has to do with how you feel about writing. While you are writing, you must believe you are creating something wonderful. You believe you are creative, witty, and smart. Your passion to reveal the truth, without bullshit, drives you to create something good.

Once you are done writing, you must discard this frame of mind. What you have created is just words on a page. Words don't love you, so why should you love them? Your job now is not to create but to reveal truth. You can rearrange, cut, or change anything that better reveals that truth. You should feel no more emotion about this than you would when pruning a shrub. You're making it better, and "it" is no longer a part of you.

This is where the second part of the trick comes in. It has to do with edits. You must not look at each suggestion and say, "Should

I do this, or should I not?" That's too binary. Worse, it means that you are judging yourself against others' thinking—are they smarter than you, or are you smarter? If accepting an edit means accepting your own imperfection, you'll resist.

Instead, you should think, "What has this suggested edit revealed about what could be better here?" This way, you remain in charge, and you remain smart. You decide what flaws the edit has revealed, even if the reviewer did not see them. You decide in what way to fix things. It might be the way the reviewer suggested, or it might be some other way. You seek a higher truth, a more profound way to communicate without bullshit.

Only in this way can you embrace criticism as a path to a better piece of writing.

This is especially difficult when you have an emotional connection to the writing. To understand what I mean, consider the parable of Ray's Helicopter.

The Parable of Ray's Helicopter

Once there was a man named Ray who was the CEO of a company that made helicopters.

In his youth, Ray had been an avid pilot. Soon after, he started the company with a few friends. Over time, Ray's Helicopter, as the company was known, grew rapidly to command an impressive share of the world market. Every day he was happy to go to work, and most days his job energized him even more. His workers respected his passion for quality and, by and large, were quite happy to work for his company.

One morning Ray's cofounder and chief of strategy visited

his office. "Ray," he said, "we need to reinforce with everyone, inside and out of our company, who we are and what we stand for. We need a statement of purpose to keep everyone inspired." Ray thought this was a good idea. Quality had always been the ideal that drove Ray and his workers, so his first thought about the purpose statement was "We make great helicopters." But Ray knew he needed his executive team's buy-in, and they would probably have other good ideas.

He visited the office of his chief operating officer. She pointed out that the company made much of its money from its extensive distribution network and service operation. So Ray changed the statement of purpose to "We make, distribute, and service great helicopters."

Then he bumped into the chief financial officer. The CFO reminded Ray that making and selling helicopters wasn't what made shareholders happy. Because the company was well managed, it made a healthy profit. So Ray added "profitably" to the statement.

He had lunch with the head of research and development, who was an old friend. She was very excited about the company's upcoming foray into the market for drones. "We don't just make helicopters anymore," she said. But the head of R&D didn't want the drones in the statement because they weren't announced yet. She and Ray settled on changing "helicopters" to "flying machines" since that covered everything they would conceivably make.

Word had begun to get around about the purpose statement. The head of human resources and the chief marketing officer showed up in his office. "We need to recognize that our strength comes from our people," said the head of HR. "And we need to get our new ad tag line in there somewhere," said the CMO. The ads for Ray's Helicopter said that the company had "machines with edge."

Finally, Ray emailed the remaining members of his executive team. His head of sales was in India with a client. He responded by saying that he couldn't get to this right away, as he was closing sales at the end of the quarter. The chief information officer didn't respond, since he didn't see how this statement affected his department. And the corporate counsel emailed back with concern about the word "great," which might be perceived as some sort of guarantee. She thought "excellent" would be a safer word.

Ray put together all the suggestions and wrote this on his whiteboard:

> At Ray's Helicopter, our global team profitably makes, distributes, and services excellent flying machines—machines with edge.

This didn't feel very inspiring, but Ray decided to think about it for a while. It was Friday evening, and he was looking forward to dinner with his wife, who had just come back from a professional conference. Talking to her always made things seem clearer to him.

They ordered dinner delivered from their favorite restaurant and sat down to dine by candlelight. Ray's wife noticed that Ray was uncharacteristically quiet and preoccupied. When she brought it up, Ray explained what had happened with the purpose statement that day.

"Ray, you started this company, and you are its heart and

soul. If you aren't happy with the statement of purpose, then you shouldn't settle. Who forced this statement on you?"

Ray was about to blame his chief of strategy but realized that he had made all the changes himself, at the suggestions of his top managers. So he really had no one to blame but himself.

"What do you really think is your purpose?" his wife asked.

"Well, we make great helicopters," he answered. "They're the greatest passenger helicopters in the world." And once he had said this, he felt much better.

He became determined to resolve the problem as soon as work started on Monday. So he called his leadership team into a meeting on Monday morning. On the whiteboard, he had written the statement from the week before:

> At Ray's Helicopter, our global team profitably makes, distributes, and services excellent flying machines—machines with edge.

"What do you think?" he asked his team. They all looked down at their smartphones and tablets and laptops. "Does this inspire you?" he prompted. Finally the CMO spoke up. "It sort of dilutes the brand," he said. "And I don't think that's the best way to use our tag line." As soon as the CMO had spoken up, the room began to buzz. It was clear that no one was satisfied with the statement.

Ray erased the statement and wrote this on the board:

> We make the greatest passenger helicopters in the world.

He could feel the mood in the room change. His cofounder

and chief of strategy was smiling. So Ray started polling his staff one by one. The chief operating officer said that the statement about being the greatest in the world would inspire the service and distribution operations, even though it didn't mention their roles by name. The head of human resources agreed that this kind of statement reflected why the workers loved working for Ray. And the head of sales said that his salespeople usually said something like this anyway, because the company made a great product. The CFO said that short-term investors looked only at the numbers and wouldn't care, and that long-term investors would probably be happy with the statement so long as the results backed it up.

The head of R&D agreed that, by far, the main product the company made or would make was helicopters, and that her best designers worked on those projects. Except for the CIO, whom nobody listened to and who rarely said anything in these meetings, this left the general counsel and the head of marketing.

Ray asked the counsel if there was any risk in this statement. "There is always risk," she said. "Anyone can sue you for anything." But she admitted to Ray that the chances of a successful suit were low because "greatest," while inspiring, is not a statement that requires proof. Ray decided this level of risk was not a problem.

The CMO still had a sour look, though. "What's the problem?" asked Ray.

"I can't help but think that our statement of purpose should have the customer in there somewhere," said the CMO.

"Who do you think is the customer?" asked Ray.

"It's the buyer," said the head of sales.

"It's the pilot," said the head of R&D.

"It's the passenger, too," said the CMO.

Could the company really have gotten so large without everyone agreeing on who the customer was? Ray doubted it. "What do these customers think of us?" Ray asked.

"The buyers love us because we create a great buying and service experience. Ours is way better than the competition," said the head of sales.

"The pilots love us because our product design keeps improving, making a better product experience for them," said the head of R&D. "We really understand flying."

"The passengers love us," said the CMO, "because we design and build the helicopters for them, not just for the pilots." He was quoting the marketing materials, but he knew it was true.

"Could we all agree that we create a great experience for buyers, pilots, and passengers?" Ray asked. Everyone nodded. ("We could call them 'stakeholders,'" said the head of HR, but her suggestion didn't catch on.)

Now the text on the board said this:

> We make the greatest passenger helicopters in the world. For buyers, for pilots, and for passengers, the Ray's Helicopter experience is the best you can get.

Ray felt a lot better now, and so did everyone else in the room. He asked the CIO to put the new text at the top of the website; the CIO said it would take three months to make the change. So Ray fired the CIO and moved the website under marketing, which was much more responsive. He also put the statement onto the company intranet and at the bottom of all his emails. Morale remained high, and the workers did all they could to live up to the promise of the purpose statement. And they all lived profitably ever after.

How to Work with Editors Without Losing Your Soul

If you ask for reviews but have no framework for using the resulting feedback, you'll be lost. That's what happened to Ray. While he was working on a very short piece of writing, it was an important one; too important to leave the editing process to chance. In the end, he took control of the process and succeeded.

This is a common problem for writers. Of the business writers in the WOBS Writing Survey who had worked on projects, about half said that they got the editorial feedback they needed to make their writing better, but only 32% said that their feedback process worked well. Writers in the survey spent an average of 19% of their project time on rewriting. You'll never succeed unless you make that big chunk of your time as efficient as possible.

If you struggle to deal with edits, keep this key principle in mind:

Editors and reviewers exist to reveal what you cannot see, not to tell you what to do.

This is a crucial distinction. If you just do everything the editor tells you to, you are not a writer, you are a stenographer.

When you are seeking and addressing feedback, follow these five steps:

1. Be clear about your vision.
2. Choose editors to match what you need.
3. Expose your flaws.

4. Use edits to gain insights.

5. Apply the insights to your rewrite.

Let's work through these steps, one by one.

Be Clear About Your Vision

If you know where you're going when you set out to write, you won't lose your way as Ray did.

Analyze your Readers, Objective, Action, and iMpression. Reflect on your target sentence as you decide how to revise.

A clear vision not only improves your writing, but also confirms your sense of direction when you receive suggestions. You're less likely to get lost if you have a map and a compass.

Choose Editors to Match What You Need

Editing is like going to the dentist—nobody likes it, but you'll avoid a lot of pain and ugliness if you get the right help at the right time. And you must pick the right intensity of editing to match what your writing needs; you can't fix a toothache with just a cleaning.

In my experience, there are five levels of edits, from spitballing big conceptual ideas to correcting nitpicky details. Apply these types of editing successively when working on a nonfiction piece of at least 2,500 words. (On shorter pieces, you can combine some levels.) Regardless of what level of review you're seeking, always set a deadline so you're not waiting around wondering where the reviews are.

Here are the five levels:

- **Idea development.** Before you start, you need an idea.

Then you need some pushback to better develop the idea. You need someone who can tell you if your idea is amazing, trite, or weak, and how you might improve it. Fixing the idea before you write saves you from wasting huge amounts of time. Write the idea out as a fat outline, then find a person or two who are great with ideas and beg them to critique the idea for 30 or 45 minutes.

- **Structural edit.** Some writers try to write from beginning to end and find themselves stuck with a bad structure or storyline. Others stitch pieces together and wonder how to make it all fit. We all end up with wonky structures and insecurity. Editors who are good with structure can help you at the fat outline stage and later when you have an early draft with some holes in it. Structural editing shouldn't scare you; it just means rearranging and combining your ideas. But it does challenge you to tell the story differently from how you've been thinking about it. Restructuring a piece of writing once or twice, regardless of the reason, inevitably makes it better because it gives you a new perspective.

- **Paragraph or line edit.** Once the storyline works, write it. Since you're not perfect, you'll have some parts that sound great and other parts full of bloated sentences, passive voice, and other flaws. Most good paragraph and line editing is cutting. Get used to seeing lots of red ink or markup. At this stage, you can also fold in comments from people with technical or legal expertise. Remember, asking for word edits on a fragmentary, incomplete draft is a waste of time. That incomplete draft is going to change a lot before you've completed it. Why bother with edits on words you won't be keeping?

- **Copyedit and fact-check.** The draft is done, sort of. But you know it's not perfect. You need copy edits and fact checks. Copyediting is a specialized skill. Copy editors can read anything and spot the inconsistencies, grammatical errors, and embarrassing word choices. They're a breed apart: They love perfection and finding little errors. Bad copy editors remove the life from language. Fight them. Good copy editors save you from your flaws. Reward them (preferably with chocolate). Fact-checking happens around this time, too. It's when you make sure that if you say News Corp owns Myspace, it's still true (actually, it isn't).

- **Proofread.** Every change you make has the potential to introduce another error. The proofread stage is when you catch those little errors. You can dispense with this stage if you've got a short piece and trust the copy editor.

Expose Your Flaws

On each draft you create, you have an idea what's wrong. Your instinct is to hide your weaknesses. That would be a mistake.

You would miss your chance to get help.

In the email that accompanies your draft, tell reviewers what you are worried about. Is the structure right? What should I cut? Have I gone too far or not far enough? What's missing? Is it "bury the lead" or "bury the lede"? Whatever you're insecure or doubtful about, let the editor know.

Be clear about what level of edit you are looking for: Do you want help with ideas, structure, content, or words?

Also point out what is not worth their effort because you know you will be fixing it later anyway.

Here's what not to include: apologies and justifications. We all know your draft is late. We know it is weaker than you hoped it would be. Good editors ignore these excuses anyway; only the content on the page matters. Why? Because the ultimate reader won't have your excuses; they'll only have what you wrote.

Use Edits to Gain Insights

The purpose of the editor is not to tell you what to do. You're the writer, and you have the vision. Their job is to show you what you cannot see. As author James McQuivey puts it: "Editors somehow have the ability to see in what you wrote something that you either didn't realize was there or were trying to set free but could not. This makes them indispensable."

An editor doing idea development can help you to clarify your vision. A structural editor can suggest frameworks in your writing that weren't visible to you. A line editor can show you what to cut to make things stronger. *But none of them know the topic the way you do.*

Nobody loves criticism. But it's a lot easier to take if your attitude is, what can I learn from this?

If you're not stuck on defending your flawed writing, you can learn a lot. This is where your vision comes in. With that vision clear in your mind, you can see which edits can make your writing more effective.

If you're not sure what a particular critique is saying, talk to the editor who shared it with you. If you make it clear that you're seeking insights, the editor will be happy to work with you.

Apply the Insights to Your Rewrite

Once you've gained the insights from your reviewers, use that knowledge to rewrite and improve your piece.

For each suggested edit or piece of advice, regardless of how big or how small, you should take one of three actions:

- Accept the edit, and do what the editor says.
- Learn from what the editor suggests, and use that knowledge to make the writing better.
- Reject the edit, but because you have a good reason.

Bad writers who are insecure accept all edits and lose control of their writing. Bad writers who are overconfident reject all edits and gain nothing from editing. Good writers consider each edit carefully, mixing all three approaches. They find ways to harmonize conflicting advice from different reviewers, a skill that often leads to a more profound truth. That's what the CEO of Ray's Helicopter did.

Some insights require a major rewrite. Knuckle down and do it. The result will be better than what you've got now.

No matter how long you've been writing, you'll never learn to love edits. But you can learn to embrace them. And that's the key to making your writing better.

19
Edit Effectively

You learned to read when you were little.

The problem is, you've been in a trance since then. You read so much, it just flows by your eyes and into your brain. And since you're mostly reading on a screen, it's even harder to concentrate. *Wake up!*

You must learn to read critically. Each time you read, your antennae should be up, looking for people whose lazy writing habits (or in some cases, evil plans) are all set to bamboozle you into believing that you read something meaningful when in fact it was bullshit.

Learn to read this way, and you'll get three benefits. You'll exercise your bullshit detector. You'll learn to spot and fix problems that also occur in your own writing. And most importantly, you'll be able to help others to write better, as an editor.

How to Edit

Editing is the most efficient thing you can do with your knowledge of writing. When you edit, you can improve a piece of writing with much less effort because someone else—the writer—does the hard work of fixing things. All good writers should edit as well.

My advice to editors is a mirror image of my advice to writers. When you get a request to review or edit something, ask the writer these questions:

- **What stage is this at?** Don't line edit the text if the writer is looking for structural feedback. And don't suggest dismantling the whole thing if it's nearly ready to be published (unless, of course, it completely sucks).
- **What are you worried about?** Ask the writer what isn't working. Keep an eye out for that as you read.
- **What's your deadline?** A great edit handed in too late is worse than worthless; it's demoralizing.
- **Why me?** The writer asked for your help for a reason— because you're good with ideas, good with words, good on the topic, or just a good sounding board. Try to live up to what the writer is seeking. If it's your technical expertise, don't concentrate on word edits.

Read the whole piece over first. What is your impression? If there are structural problems, concentrate on those—suggest a structure, and don't line edit. If there are conceptual problems, explain what has confused you, and suggest a solution.

If it's in pretty good shape, go back and make specific suggestions. To make the writer's life a lot easier, use the Word or Google Docs markup features, not ink on paper. Highlight passages that are confusing. Suggest reordering sentences. Don't just identify passive voice, weasel words, and jargon; suggest rewrites.

And always, always identify what to cut. Shorter is better.

Finally, suggest a better title, if you have one, and a better opening sentence or two.

Now it's time to present your suggestions to the writer. Here is where you take advantage of the well-known principle of the criticism sandwich (also colloquially known as the "shit sandwich"). Surround the criticism with praise before and after. You can deliver your review in person, or by email with an attachment or link for the marked-up draft.

Start by reinforcing what's working well: "This is a great idea," or "This inspired me," or "I loved how clearly structured this piece was." Starting with praise, rather than criticism, defuses the writer's natural tendency to be defensive.

Then give a summary of the problems: "There was a lot of passive voice here," or "It's just too long, so I suggested some places to cut." Having set the writer up with praise, now you need to be clear about what to fix. Both of you can concentrate on the text rather than on the writer's personal qualities.

Finish with something positive and hopeful: "These are serious problems, but I know they are fixable and you can fix them. That will make the main idea much clearer and more powerful." Being hopeful at the end helps the writer face the job ahead with optimism and energy.

Finding pleasure in the misfortune of others—Schadenfreude—is completely normal. It's one of the joys of editing. Just try not to show it in front of the person you're editing. You'll both be happier, and the results will be better (and the writer will learn more).

Now let's look at some specific problems in writing and how to fix them.

Writing Too Long

How you notice it: You're reading a piece and start thinking, "When are they going to get to the point?" or "This is the same point again; is there anything new here?"

Question to ask yourself: What's essential here, and what's redundant?

What advice to give the writer: Identify and combine repeated or extraneous points. Cut and reorganize efficiently.

For further detail: See chapter 4.

Author Has Buried the Lede

How you notice it: A little ways into the piece, you say to yourself, "Ah, now I see what this is about."

Question to ask yourself: What is the point of this piece of writing? What title and opener would get that across quickly?

What advice to give the writer: Cut opening paragraphs. Suggest new title.

For further detail: See chapter 5.

Passive Voice Sentences

How you notice it: You get an uneasy feeling that things are happening or are supposed to happen, but you can't tell who is doing them. The writing seems disconnected from reality.

Question to ask yourself: Who is doing things here?

What advice to give the writer: Rewrite passive sentences with the actor as subject in the sentence.

For further detail: See chapter 6.

Too Much Jargon

How you notice it: You're reading the words but can't figure out what the heck they mean.

Question to ask yourself: What is the author trying to say?

What advice to give the writer: Choose a few key terms and define them. Rewrite the rest of the text using simpler words that the whole audience will understand.

For further detail: See chapter 7.

Too Many Weasel Words

How you notice it: Sentences appear to say something, but on closer examination, everything is hedged and qualified.

Question to ask yourself: What actual, definite truths could replace the qualified sentences?

What advice to give the writer: Gird your loins, stop qualifying, and tell the truth. Replace qualifying words such as "very" with statistics or verifiable statements about subgroups.

For further detail: See chapter 8.

Writing Lacks Clear Advice

How you notice it: Statements exist in a vacuum and seem indirect.

Question to ask yourself: Who is the audience? What are they supposed to be doing?

What advice to give the writer: Rewrite sentences using "you," "I," and "we." Take responsibility for the advice you're giving the reader. Suggest direct actions to take.

For further detail: See chapter 9.

Imprecise Use of Numbers

How you notice it: The writing includes numbers, but it's not clear what they mean or where they came from.

Question to ask yourself: What is the significance of these numbers?

What advice to give the writer: Include sources, and make sure all numbers have a context—something to compare them with.

For further detail: See chapter 10.

Lack of Structure and Skimmability

How you notice it: Everything is written in a series of paragraphs.

Question to ask yourself: Are there elements of this that have a clear structure?

What advice to give the writer: Rewrite with subheads, bullets, numbered lists, tables, or graphics.

For further detail: See chapter 11.

It's Not Clear Why the Piece Even Exists

How you notice it: You find yourself asking, "Why am I reading this?"

Question to ask yourself: Who is the audience? What's the author's objective, and what action do they expect the reader to take?

What advice to give the writer: Do a ROAM analysis.

For further detail: See chapter 13.

There's No Central Idea

How you notice it: You can't figure out what holds the piece together.

Question to ask yourself: How do the ideas here relate to a central idea?

What advice to give the writer: Conduct a brainstorming session to identify the key idea.

For further detail: See chapter 15.

Writing Is Choppy

How you notice it: The tone is inconsistent.

Question to ask yourself: What is this writer's process?

What advice to give the writer: Prepare first and do research before writing. Set aside a sacred writing time. Learn what flow feels like.

For further detail: See chapters 12 and 16.

Writing Is a Pastiche

How you notice it: There's a central idea and focus, but other elements seem added on or contradictory.

Question to ask yourself: Where did these extra elements come from?

What advice to give the writer: Take control of your review process. Solicit feedback, but manage how and when you use it.

For further detail: See chapters 17 and 18.

Part Four

Change What You Produce

20
Understand Containers

We worry too much about the containers that writing comes in and not enough about the writing itself.

People obsess over how they format their email and to whom they will send it. They fiddle with the margins and footnotes in their reports. This effort is counterproductive.

Writing is writing. The themes of this book—being direct, avoiding unnecessary words, and above all, the Iron Imperative to treat the reader's time as more valuable than your own— apply no matter when you write, for whom you write, and how you publish.

Fifty years ago, Marshall McLuhan said, "The medium is the message." It's still true. While the container—the email, the blog post, the press release, or the report—matters far less than the writing within it, it *does* matter. Each container comes with a load of expectations about how to consume what's within it.

Containers Carry Connotations

Email generates expectations. You can forward it, reply to it, archive it, or delete it. Email is ephemeral—we don't expect people to keep it around, even if we worry that they might keep it and hold it against us. Like a person shouting in a crowd, an email arrives in a blizzard of other emails and must spread its message amid the noise. And now that there are messaging systems built into social media, even the word "email" is spreading into a broader messaging space, in which each type of message has its own connotations.

Social media has conventions. It tends to be public, to enable comments, and to spread virally. Posts are short; tweets are shorter. Writers make social posts to get noticed, which changes how readers interpret a post and how they react to it.

Marketing communications is in flux. People still send press releases. But what is a press release now? Who gets it? How do they treat it differently from an email? And in what ways do marketers communicate beyond the traditional release? We need a new set of rules.

When corporate workers want to make a big impact with sustained effort, they write a report or white paper. Unlike readers of the other containers I've mentioned here, report readers expect research, excellent formatting, graphics, and executive summaries. Reports also provide ample spaces for bullshit to flourish since they can be arbitrarily long.

Business writers write for a variety of different types of containers (see figure 13). Each container comes with its own connotations. Regardless of the container, you should be brief and bold. You should front-load your content, avoid qualifiers, and develop ideas with a systematic process. But you can't be effective unless you account for the connotations of the container you're writing in.

In the chapters that follow, I'll look more deeply into the con-

FIGURE 13. Containers that business writers write for.

What people write for work (business writers)

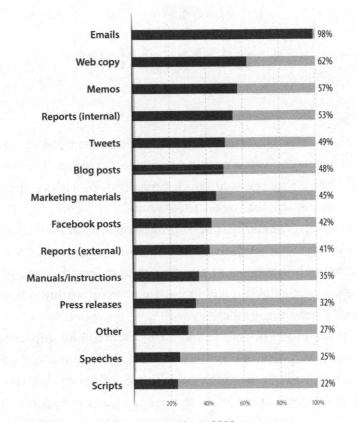

Container	Percentage
Emails	98%
Web copy	62%
Memos	57%
Reports (internal)	53%
Tweets	49%
Blog posts	48%
Marketing materials	45%
Facebook posts	42%
Reports (external)	41%
Manuals/instructions	35%
Press releases	32%
Other	27%
Speeches	25%
Scripts	22%

Source: WOBS Writing Survey, January–March 2016.
Base: 547 business professionals who write in English two or more hours per week, excluding email.

tainers that writing comes in and the connotations they generate. I'll show you a ROAM analysis for each one to ground your writing in that format. And I'll give you those extra bits of advice that can make you effective in writing for whatever container you've chosen.

21
Email Thoughtfully

Email is so common that we typically don't even think about it. Writing emails is like munching on popcorn; we just do it mindlessly. To get what we want: think, type, send. Or if it's a response to another email: read, react, type, send.

It's so unconscious that, according to researcher Linda Stone, 80% of us actually cease our normal breathing patterns while reading and answering emails. She calls it "email apnea." It's tough to be thoughtful and impactful in your writing if you're not even breathing properly.

The sum total of your emails makes more of an impression than anything else you do at work—and takes up more of your time. Respondents in the WOBS Writing Survey say they spend an average of 9.3 hours per week reading emails and another 6.4 hours per week writing them. The Radicati Group estimates that the average businessperson sends or receives 121 emails per day.

If you're going to stand out in that cramped, noisy environment, you'll need to be thoughtful about how best to accomplish your goals with email.

Email Purposefully

Emailing on automatic pilot is easy. You write a subject line, type what occurs to you, add as many people as you can think of to the "To:" line, and then hit Send. It's the quickest thing you can write.

By writing thoughts in the order they come to you, you save yourself time but make your reader work harder. By including extra recipients, you take up even more people's time. You've violated the Iron Imperative: You've treated your own time as more important than the reader's. And you're doing it multiple times a day.

A hastily composed email often becomes what I call "the puzzler." You know, the email that recipients read and say, "Why did I get this? What am I supposed to do about it?" The busy person puts it aside and then forgets about it, which means the sender needs to follow up. That wastes time. Or the recipient asks for clarification and copies everyone else, which wastes even more people's time.

Rethink emails. The first instinct you need to change is that email is the solution to all problems. Get up and talk to people. Call them on the phone. If it's an issue that would benefit from dialogue, email is not the best way to solve it.

If you do decide to send an email, recognize that there are two types of emails: those that are important to you and the recipient, and those that are not. Important emails include emails you send to groups of customers or employees, as well as those that you send to one person to generate action. Important emails are important enough to plan and execute thoughtfully, and I'm about to show you how to do that, quickly.

What about the unimportant emails? You can save yourself a lot of time on those. *Just don't send them.* You'll be better off and so will the people whose inboxes you won't be clogging up.

ROAM Analysis of an Email

If it's worth writing, it's worth analyzing with ROAM (check chapter 13 if you need a refresher). So what's the ROAM analysis of an email?

- **Readers: a precise group of people.** Figure out who you need to act on the email. Include them, and only them, on the list of recipients. Don't cover your ass by writing to more people. And don't use corporate mailing lists unless you know who's on them; sometimes "North America Sales" goes to 750 random people, many of whom will just be annoyed by your irrelevant message. Don't use the Cc field if you can help it, and don't ever use the Bcc field (blind copy)—it's deceitful and can come back to bite you if one of the recipients reveals what you were trying to hide.
- **Objective: get an answer or spread information.** Are you asking or telling? If you're asking, be clear about what you need. If you're telling, be clear about what you're sharing and why. If you don't *know* why you're sending the email, *don't send it.*
- **Action: what you hope will happen next.** If you're asking for information, then the action you want is a helpful response. Include a deadline. If you're sharing information, what do you want the recipient to do about it? If you can't answer that, *don't send the email.*
- **iMpression: sound effective.** Asking for precise informa-

tion for a specific purpose shows that you're doing your job. Telling people what you need them to do and why, clearly and briefly, also makes a positive impression. Rambling on aimlessly doesn't. So be brief, well organized, and clear.

For an email requesting action, the resulting target sentence is this:

After reading my email, the recipients will understand what I need, send it to me, and perceive me as efficient.

And for an email spreading information, the target sentence is similarly simple:

After reading my email, the recipients will understand the information I've shared, act on it, and perceive me as providing valuable information.

Anatomy of an Effective Email

Emails look unstructured. They're not. Each email tells a story that looks like this: Here's who I am; here's what's happening; here's what it means; here's what you should do. The key for all these parts is brevity and clarity. It's the perfect place to say just what you mean.

Here's a quick checklist on what to include:

- **A subject line that's clear about what you need.** For example, use something like "2016 attrition statistics for your review" if you're just sharing information, or "Would like your help tracking down a logistics expert" if you're asking for help. Put the "ask" in the subject line. People are in a hurry and will otherwise miss it.

- **A microwave greeting.** If the recipient doesn't know you, warm things up with the fastest possible introduction, like "I'm a colleague of Alan's in our finance department."

- **A one-sentence summary.** Don't start with an apology or a comment about the local baseball team. Your first substantive sentence should tell the whole story. If the recipient doesn't read the whole email, they'll at least get something from the subject line and this sentence. For example, "I can't complete my year-end books until I get your accounting of consulting expenses."

- **The facts, on one topic only, structured for browsing.** Put separate topics in separate emails, even if you're targeting the same list of recipients. Otherwise, you'll mess up people who forward the email or classify it as an item on their to-do lists. And remember, you've got 100 to 250 words before your recipient, who is probably reading on a smartphone, gets bored. Be brief. Boomerang, which provides tools for better email productivity, found in a study that longer emails get lower response rates, with the decline starting at a length of 100 words. Use the skimmable features I described in chapter 11: bullets, paragraph leads in bold type, even graphics. (Skip the tables; they render poorly.) If you must include more detail, link to documents on the web or your corporate intranet, or if absolutely necessary, include an attachment.

- **The call to action with a deadline.** If you want the recipient to act, say so at the end with a more specific "ask" than what was in the subject line. For example, "Please get back to me with an estimate by tomorrow."

- **Thank you, and goodbye.** Once you've finished, get off the stage. And remember, your signature is part of your message. We just need your name, phone number, and email address, not a baroque listing of everything you've ever done with graphical filigrees.

Here's an example: The *Boston Globe* was in crisis in January 2016. It had just switched delivery suppliers, and the customers were upset. The new supplier was failing to deliver papers to between 5% and 10% of them. I showed you the *Globe* publisher's apology in chapter 3. Now have a look at the email that Scott Steeves—head of the *Globe*'s union, the Boston Newspaper Guild—sent to ask everyone who worked there, including reporters, to help deliver the paper:

From: Scott Steeves
To: [All Boston Globe staff]
Subject: Help Needed Tonight

Dear Members—
We are in crisis mode. I'm sure you've all heard about the papers not getting delivered this past week. We are looking for people to work tonight delivering papers in the Newton area. Anyone from the editorial side who is able to work tonight delivering papers, please email Beth Healy. Anyone from the business side who is able to work tonight delivering papers, please contact Scott Steeves.
   We will be meeting at 15 Riverdale Ave. in Newton at midnight. Globe employees will need to be two per car. Please have proof of driver's license and registration. You

will get a route with a list of households with delivery in-structions. Make sure you have a flashlight and a GPS.

Appreciate everybody who can help out. Thanks in advance.

There is no vacillating apology here. The subject line is "Help Needed" (passive voice, but hey, nobody's perfect). After that, "We are in crisis mode. I'm sure you've all heard about the papers not getting delivered," is a pretty clear statement of the problem. And then Steeves asks for help and provides clear instructions. The whole thing is 132 words long.

And it worked, too. In an unprecedented scene, a bunch of re-porters gathered in the wee hours in Newton, Massachusetts, set out to deliver the Sunday edition of the *Boston Globe,* and made a big difference to its readers.

The Cold Email: Getting Help from Someone You Don't Know

In chapter 14, I talked about lining up research interviews. Now I'm going to share my road-tested email strategy that yields those interviews.

It includes all the elements I just described—a clear ask in the subject line, a microwave greeting, clarity about what the sender needs, and next steps. But I add two more elements in line with the Iron Imperative.

First, I send each email individually and customize it. Sure, it would be easier to email a bunch of contacts at once. But an in-dividual email shows the person who you want to interview that you know who you're emailing. To make this work, I reference the past relationship I've had with the recipient and show respect for their work, without being a sycophant.

Second, I explain how our contact will benefit the recipient, to justify why it is worth the time to answer my email.

For example, here's the email I sent to get Richard Edelman, CEO of the major global communications and marketing firm that bears his name, to participate in an interview for this book:

From: Josh Bernoff
To: Richard Edelman
Subject: Would like to interview you for my book

Richard:
I'm completing my book on clear and powerful communication, due out from HarperBusiness in 2016. (I left Forrester in March of 2015.)

I've always been impressed by your perspectives, including when you presented at the Forrester conference a few years ago.

I'd like to get a commonsense quote or two from you in there regarding press releases, blog posts, and what makes sense now for PR practitioners and other marketers writing in the social media age.

Can we set up 30 minutes or so to talk in the first week of January? I'd be very grateful for your help.

Thanks,
Josh
=============================
Josh Bernoff
WOBS, LLC

That's 115 words. The ask is in the subject line. My microwave greeting is 22 words. I suggest that I'll quote him. And I include a deadline.

I don't talk about phone numbers, dates, and times I'm available, or whether the interview is on the record, or why this is going to be the greatest book ever published. I know Richard Edelman is busy and doesn't want to read that crap. He has to decide if speaking with me is worthwhile. I give him enough information to make that decision, and if he says yes to that or asks a question, I'm ready to respond.

I sent this email out on New Year's Day 2016 and got an answer before the start of the first working day of the year.

If you don't have a recipient's email address, you can contact these people through social network messaging, as I'll describe in chapter 22.

The Marketing Email: Generating Action

There are whole books and thousands of blog posts dedicated to marketing emails, the ones that marketers send en masse to their contact and customer lists. You know, the ones that end up in the Promotions tab in your Gmail—the ones that you sometimes look at and usually skip.

You can smell them a mile away because they're usually trying to sell you something.

Over 10 million marketers send a total of more than a billion emails a month using MailChimp. As of January 2016, the typical "open rate"—the proportion of emails that recipients actually view—ranges from a high of 29% (for emails about hobbies) to a low of 14% (for emails about daily deals). Of every 100 mass emails that MailChimp's users send, people open around 20, depending on the subject. It's pathetic.

Your ad agency can help you play this cat-and-mouse game. Or you can decide to do things a little differently.

Start with ROAM, and focus on your objective. What are you trying to do? "Get people to buy" isn't good enough. "Increase my open rate" is lame. How about "Remind people preparing for the Christmas rush that we can help them with seasonal workers"? Or "Show them what fun videos we create, so when they need to make a video, they'll call us"?

Continue with the Iron Imperative. Shar VanBoskirk, who has been studying marketing email effectiveness at Forrester Research for over a decade, explains that "the best programs are ones that balance business goals with user needs." That means that your email must treat the customer's time as a valuable commodity. Don't just give them a reason to open your email. Give them a reason to *be glad* they opened it.

Here's how:

- **Use a short, descriptive subject line.** Brevity rules in marketing emails. "Time to buy a new suit" might not get too many opens, but it's going to hit the man who has been thinking he needs a new suit. At the end of 2015, Angie's List emailed me about "5 Kitchen Backsplash Trends for 2016." That's boring . . . unless you're remodeling your kitchen, at which point it becomes fascinating.
- **Keep the text short.** Write no more than three to five lines of text. If you get recipients to look at your email at all, they'll

probably be looking at it on a smartphone. Emails that you have to scroll are far less effective.

- **Write like a person.** We don't want to hear from marketers. Even if the email is from a corporate account, write as someone at the company directly to the customer. According to Ann Handley, author of the marketer's writing book *Everybody Writes,* "[Marketing email] content should feel as if it comes from an actual person, speaking to me in the first person (use *I* or *we* and *you*) with natural-sounding language."
- **Use small graphics or images, but only if they're relevant.** A picture of the nice room in your bed-and-breakfast is effective and helpful. A generic sunset isn't.
- **Don't wear out your welcome.** I once bought some Hanes underwear online. Hanes started to email me once a week. I don't buy new underwear weekly. I unsubscribed in a hurry.

Help the customer, and you can do just about anything. For example, Kraft Foods allows people to sign up for a daily recipe email, sent in the afternoon, with tips on what to shop for. Busy working parents use it to figure out what to pick up on the way home and cook that evening. Kraft gets to remind people of its brands because they're helpful, and the recipients *willingly* sign up for daily emails—something Hanes could only dream of.

If you're clear about the action you're seeking and the benefit you're offering, this becomes much easier. Use the subject line to highlight what they'll get. Explain it in the first few lines in the body of the email. And make it easy for the reader to click and get the benefit. You'll reach the customers who matter, regardless of the open rate.

The Managerial Email: Sharing News Efficiently

There is no form of email that has more potential for bullshit than the email from a manager—such as a CEO, a division head, or an HR leader—to a large group of employees. Remember Stephen Elop's 1,100-word email from chapter 4—the one that buried the news about laying off 12,500 people until 80% of the way through?

I think the reason these emails go wrong so often is that no one who might review them ahead of time is willing to point out that the boss is about to screw up.

If you're the manager sending this type of email, here are my recommendations:

- **Email your people regularly.** Monthly or quarterly is a good rhythm. You'll get better at it, and your people will get used to it.
- **Keep each missive under 400 words.** And stick to one topic, such as a product launch, a strategic shift, or a merger. (Managers violate the one-topic rule all the time because topics run together in their minds. But you're there to make your staff efficient, not the other way around.)
- **Don't bury the lede.** If there's bad news, don't hide it; just come out with it. Tongues will start wagging as soon as people figure it out, so you may as well be blunt.
- **Dump the management-speak.** Leaders often feel the need to adopt and use the jargon ("magic words") from the company strategy. Your staff will pay lip service if you use this jargon, but they'll perceive you as a bullshitter. Far better to

explain how you and your staff must live these imperatives than just to slather your email with "cloud-based" this and "disruptive innovation" that.

- **Get edits from somebody who will stand up to you.** If you're surrounded by yes-men, they won't tell you that you're about to look like an idiot. Find somebody who can tell you that you're about to insult the staff, fling too much jargon, write in the passive voice, or just use too many words. Then take those edits to heart.

Here's an example of how a manager can effectively share news—even bad news. Twitter cofounder Jack Dorsey had just returned to the company as CEO and needed to make some changes—and some cuts. He sent this email to his workforce when he needed to cut 8% of his staff. (In case you're not a Twitter expert, the capitalized words are all product names.)

From: Jack Dorsey
To: All Employees
Date: October 13, 2015
Subject: A more focused Twitter

Team,
We are moving forward with a restructuring of our workforce so we can put our company on a stronger path to grow. Emails like this are usually riddled with corporate speak so I'm going to give it to you straight.

The team has been working around the clock to produce [a] streamlined roadmap for Twitter, Vine, and Periscope and they are shaping up to be strong. The roadmap is focused on the experiences which will have the greatest impact. We launched the first of these experiences last week with Moments, a great beginning, and a bold peek into the future of how people will see what's going on in the world.

The roadmap is also a plan to change how we work, and what we need to do that work. Product and Engineering are going to make the most significant structural changes to reflect our plan ahead. We feel strongly that Engineering will move much faster with a smaller and nimbler team, while remaining the biggest percentage of our workforce. And the rest of the organization will be streamlined in parallel.

So we have made an extremely tough decision: we plan to part ways with up to 336 people from across the company. We are doing this with the utmost respect for each and every person. Twitter will go to great lengths to take care of each individual by providing generous exit packages and help finding a new job.

Let's take this time to express our gratitude to all of those who are leaving us. We will honor them by doing our best to serve all the people that use Twitter. We do so with a more purpose-built team, which we'll continue to build strength into over time, as we are now enabled to reinvest in our most impactful priorities.

Thank you all for your trust and understanding here. This isn't easy. But it is right. The world needs a strong Twitter, and this is another step to get there. As always, please reach out to me directly with any ideas or questions.

Jack

That's 348 words. Regarding the layoff, it's clear but not cruel or insensitive, starting with the subject line "A more focused Twitter." It explains management's reasoning without downplaying the necessity.

Etiquette Tips for Email Without Bullshit

An awful lot has been written about email etiquette. I'll stick to what I think is new and crucial in the smartphone era.

The Right Tone Is Business Casual

Just as in many workplaces you no longer need to wear a suit, tie, or dress, you also don't need to exaggerate the formality of the business relationship in email.

In a business casual email, you can use colloquial expressions and metaphors. You can and should use direct, active statements and requests. You should use numbers. And remember, "please" is not a weasel word—when you need help, say "please."

I recognize, as well, that some emails require delicacy because they deal with emotional issues (such as a critique of a person's behavior). But sensitivity and directness are not contradictory. Include the facts, but not just the facts. Address the emotional issues without apologizing. You'll find that a small dab of sensitivity goes a long way, while a large dollop is unprofessional and counterproductive.

Regardless of how you or your readers feel, do not use profanity, exclamation points, emojis, or emoticons such as ":-)". In my experience, workers who use these sorts of over-friendly affectations are trying to smooth over difficulties they've had or requests they need to make. We're grownups here. At work, we ask each other for stuff. When we mess up, we say so. Younger staff should recognize that they're not in college anymore and should learn to be friendly and direct without being cute.

Don't Compose Email on a Smartphone

Why do you use your smartphone for email? It's because you've got spaces in your day and you'd like to get a little work done and cut back on the backlog. And, let's face it, it's because you have a smartphone habit that you can't kick.

It's fine to *read* email on your smartphone. It's even fine to *respond* to email on your smartphone. Just don't create anything important there.

Writing email that doesn't waste the reader's time requires thought and planning. It takes editing, too. Your smartphone doesn't support thought, planning, and editing very well. Compose important emails on a computer.

Respect the Hierarchy

You're going to need to email your boss, or your boss's boss. This scares some people, but it shouldn't. This is exactly where the clarity and brevity you've learned will pay off.

Bosses want respect, information, and truth. Be clear about who you are, why you're emailing, what happened, and what you recommend. Don't tell bosses what to do; don't dump a problem on them without a recommendation, either.

It's not a coincidence that this is the same advice that applies to other emails. Once you master the habit of effective email, that habit succeeds regardless of the recipient.

When Responding, Respect Recipients' Time

I can't leave the topic of email without discussing how to respond to email—especially since the flurry of email responses is what accounts for the overwhelming clutter. My rule here is simple: the fewer, shorter responses you can make, the better. Here's how to do that:

- **Read the most recent messages first.** Then if someone else has taken care of the problem, you can skip it. Don't waste recipients' time replying to messages they've already dealt with.
- **Get in the habit of replying only to the sender.** I've trained myself to hit Reply rather than Reply All. This cuts down enormously on "Cc: clutter" in other people's inboxes. (It also protects you from the classic and totally embarrassing Reply All gaffe in which you inadvertently spam a hundred people with your reply.) In any modern email system, if you want to switch the response to Reply All after composing but before sending, you can.
- **If you have nothing to say, say nothing.** Not replying works just as well as "I don't know." Why clutter others' inboxes with a proclamation of your ignorance?
- **If no answer is required, say nothing.** There's no need to respond to informational messages unless you have an additional observation that others can benefit from.
- **If you have an answer to a question, be brief.** If you're responding to an email sent only to you, send a complete answer. But if the email went to a group, others will find it tedious to read your long answer. Long and winding chains of responses can get out from under the original topic, re-

sulting in a detailed discussion of marketing strategy hidden under the subject heading "Last Sunday's golf outing." Share your short answer, or begin a new, carefully composed email to share your longer observations.

- **And finally, consider just talking to people.** If the email chain has gone back and forth three or four times, you can be the one to save people's time. Pick up the phone. Walk down the hall. And solve the problem with a conversation.

22

Master Social Media

When Charlene Li and I wrote our book on social media, *Groundswell,* in 2008, we thought social media would change everything. We wanted to prepare businesses to live in a conversational world—a world where every act of marketing, corporate communication, and customer service included both talking and listening.

It didn't turn out that way.

True, social media has transformed our experience of the world. Facebook, in particular, has an outsize influence on what people read. But despite a whole lot of lip service to the *idea* of conversational marketing, marketers focus their efforts on one-way activities like advertising and static web pages.

What a missed opportunity.

The containers that hold two-way conversational writing—blogs, social networks, and messaging systems—are versatile. They include text, graphics, photos, videos, and calls to action. They connect with people, not just as an undifferentiated audience, but individually. And they can spread. If you do conversational content right, your own customers will spread your message beyond the reach of any advertisement you could buy—and for free.

To boost your career, you must master the containers that create conversation.

So let's talk about four tools that you really ought to master: blogs, social networks, messaging, and corporate social spaces.

Blog Profitably

The blogosphere contains more bullshit, taken together, than any other collection of media on the planet. Unless you live in China or Iran, there is no censorship. Any moron, anywhere, can post anything. And they do.

Should this scare you away? Nope. It's an opportunity. Create the right content, and the world will come pouring in. It's a popular idea; half the writers I surveyed said they wrote blog posts.

Here's the basic equation for business blogging. You write something useful. People hear about it. They spread it. Lots of folks come to read your blog. While they're there, they think, "Wow, this is useful." They learn about whatever it is you have to offer, and they buy it (or at least consider buying it). And they tell their friends.

These blogs are also part of "content marketing"—winning people over by providing helpful content. But let's put the buzzwords aside and see how it works. I'll speak here from personal experience.

In early 2015, I started a blog about clear writing at without bullshit.com. On Monday, May 4, 2015, I wrote an 1,100-word post called "10 Top Writing Tips and the Psychology Behind Them." I also included a little chart of my ten tips (you saw it in chapter 11).

The post received over 6,000 views the first day, which was more than double my previous best day. Then it started spreading, because people found it useful and interesting.

By Friday of that week, it was up to 56,000 views per day. Over 10,000 people had shared it on Facebook, and 10,000 more on Twitter. After several weeks it tapered off, but as I write this, eight months later, it still generates 300 to 500 views per day.

Not only that, as of this writing, if you search for "writing tips" on Google, it's one of the top three results.

What good did all that do me?

Now that two-thirds of a million people have read the post, a lot more people know my name.

Several thousand have subscribed to my blog, so I'm in touch with them.

All this—the popular post, the Google ranking, the subscriptions—puts me in an ideal position to market what I have to market: services and books.

Any blog post can find its audience, just as mine did, and take off. It's a question of being useful to the customers you're trying to reach.

The ROAM Analysis of a Blog

Prospective bloggers tend to start with the wrong question: Which blogging platform should I use? They remind me of Mr. Anchovy, the timid chartered accountant in a Monty Python sketch who yearns to be a lion tamer. When his vocational guidance counselor points out how ill-suited Mr. Anchovy is for lion taming, Anchovy points out that he's all set because he has *a lion-taming hat.*

If you want to take up taming lions, you don't start by buying the hat. And if you want to take up blogging, you don't start by talking about platforms, frequency, or fonts. You start by asking why. You start, as you should start any writing project, with a ROAM analysis.

- Readers: potential and current customers.
- Objective: to make those customers smarter.
- Action: readers should subscribe to your blog, share it, and check out your products.
- iMpression: readers should think of your company as expert and helpful.

Here's the resulting target sentence:

> After reading this blog post, potential and current customers will learn something, share our blog, check out our products and services, and think of our company as helpful.

The hard part of this is figuring out how you will help your blog readers. You have to stop thinking about yourself (nobody wants to hear about you) and start putting yourself in the shoes of your reader. Here's how to get started:

- **Cue up a few ideas.** You'll have more impact if you've thought through a bunch of useful things you could be posting. Perhaps your first post will be a hit, but the odds are against it. You're more likely to meet your objectives with a series of useful posts.
- **Pick a location that fits your audience and frequency.** Medium and LinkedIn are ideal platforms for the occasional

blogger; you can get started quickly without worrying about formatting or hosting issues. If you're going to blog regularly, you can establish a reputation with a contributed blog at *Forbes* or the *Huffington Post*. Use WordPress—and get some design and development help—to set up a blog on your own site. If your company has already set up a blog platform, use that. It's not the format you should worry about, it's the content.

- **Spend extra time on titles and first sentences.** Blogs are front-loaded. They either hook you in the first few sentences, or they fail. That title and those sentences will also appear in Google results. They'll attract more attention if they describe the content brilliantly and promise more.

- **Deliver meaty, structured content.** Use all the tips from chapters 4 through 11: your blog should include bullets, lists, graphics, subheads, and active, direct, jargon-free text featuring "I" and "you." Include links to other useful blogs and content. Blogs are informal; people expect you to speak to them directly.

- **Include a graphic worth sharing.** Every post should have a graphic, not only because it breaks up the march of paragraphs but also because it will appear in Facebook links. Shareable graphics are a powerful way to accomplish your blog objectives. Jeremiah Owyang, influential observer of technology-driven trends and prolific blogger, is great at this. A few years ago, when he was an analyst at Altimeter Group, one graphic he posted about career paths for corporate social media strategists got viewed over 30,000 times (see figure 14). (Owyang went on to found a company called Crowd Companies, building on his expertise on the shar-

FIGURE 14. Jeremiah Owyang's social media career graphic for Altimeter Group.

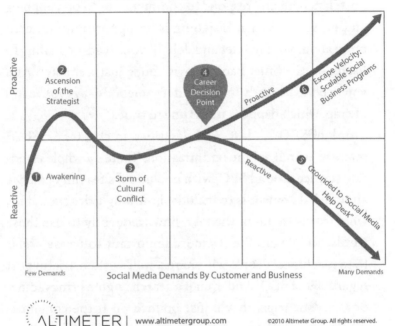

The Two Career Paths of the Corporate Social Strategist

Source: Altimeter Group, a Prophet Company.

ing economy; Altimeter Group was acquired and is now a Prophet Company.) When you publish shareable graphics, make sure they include links back to your site, so they keep working for you even when they're ripped from their context in your blog.

- **Promote on social media.** Post links to your blog posts on Twitter, Facebook, and LinkedIn. Or make friends with popular people on social media, and ask them to help promote. In companies with established blogs, the public relations staff may be responsible for promoting your post, but don't assume—check.

- **Listen and respond.** This is *conversational* media. Don't just post; listen for and respond to comments, both on your blog and on social media. Listening is an opportunity to learn more about your market and delight your readers. Failing to listen, on the other hand, shows you're just a shouter. And you need to be ready to respond if somebody says you're full of crap, which happens from time to time.

- **Think of SEO . . . last.** As I described in chapter 5, "SEO" refers to search engine optimization. There's a whole elaborate science around SEO, with books and sites full of advice about what keywords to include, how long titles should be, what words to put in the text, how frequently to use those words, and so on. But it's more important to please *people* than machines. People will share a well-written, useful post regardless of SEO. And even if a search engine brings someone to your page, they'll just bounce off if the content is wordy, rambling, and useless.

Post Frequently on Social Networks

In the WOBS Writing Survey, 49% of business writers said they tweeted for work, and 42% said they wrote Facebook posts. Along with LinkedIn, these are valuable social channels that can spread useful ideas for work. How should you exploit them?

First off, take stock of your assets. If you (or your company) have a lot of followers and friends in these spaces, there's an opportunity to spread your word more broadly. Even if you don't, social networks create a place where you can initiate dialogue and learn.

The ROAM Analysis of Social Networks

Put simply, you use social networks to spread your ideas. Here's the ROAM analysis:

- **Readers: your public following.** Your readers are your friends and followers or those of your company, as well as others who will be interested in what you have to say.
- **Objective: get these followers to embrace a message.** Use social networks to get people to know more about the positions you champion, your useful products, or your awesome insights.
- **Action: share and click.** The most valuable thing a social network can do is spread your message broadly. It's free advertising if what you write catches on.
- **iMpression: you're worth following.** You'd like to leave people impressed with your ideas and products.

The target sentence for social network posts looks like this:

After reading what you post on social networks, friends and followers will embrace your messages by sharing what you've written, and think of you or your company as worth following.

Once you've established yourself as useful, you can throw in something overtly promotional once in a while, but if you promote yourself too frequently, you'll lose the following you built up.

The target sentence tells you what you should be posting: things that spread. That means your content must be short, no more than three or four sentences. It should be front-loaded, with something fascinating at the top to get people interested. It should include a link for people who want to go further: this is your opportunity to help people to understand what you do. And it should include a graphic, because social networks allocate more space to posts with graphics, and people are more likely to notice them and click on them.

Above all, your post should be useful. People spread useful things. By spreading useful content, you're obeying the Iron Imperative; you're treating the reader's time as more valuable than your own.

You won't succeed on social networks unless you post at least a few times a week. You can share content from others or links to media—you don't need to create your own great stuff daily. But if you only poke your head up every month or two, you'll lack visibility and credibility when you do appear. If you're posting from a corporate account, your company's social media team should be responsible for the posting schedule.

I've left out a key bit here: How do you build up an audience? It's an important question, but I have neither the space nor the expertise to describe the detailed tactics. Check out Guy Kawasaki and Peg Fitzpatrick's *The Art of Social Media* or the blogs at Hubspot.com for an endless supply of up-to-date suggestions.

Choose Social Networks Based on Their Characteristics and Your Needs

All the social networks worth your time have now converged on a similar concept featuring followers, a feed, links, and messaging. Despite the similarities, they have widely varying audiences and potential. Here's a breakdown of how they compare as I write this in 2016:

Facebook has the greatest potential, but the most inscrutable algorithm. Facebook hosts far more social activity than any other platform. It spreads text posts, links, pictures, and videos; everything viral goes through Facebook. But Facebook's master algorithm for deciding who sees what is secret and ever changing. It's like a prosperous kingdom ruled by a benevolent autocrat who changes his mind—and the laws—at random intervals. You can promote stuff on your corporate page with paid advertising, use a personal account (limited to 5,000 friends), or create an opt-in group. One element of the mysterious algorithm is clear, though: If you can get a few people to like and comment on your posts, they'll spread; otherwise, they'll become invisible.

Twitter works if you're popular—and brief. Kim Kardashian, Lady Gaga, and some media properties like TV networks have active Twitter audiences in the millions. If you or your company have an account like this, take advantage of it. But Twitter feeds are so cluttered that even if you have a huge follower count and repost tweets several times per day, many of your followers won't see them. Twitter is best for links and photos, which can spread rapidly if they're relevant and witty. Respect the 140-character limitation. Brevity is the soul of Twit.

LinkedIn reaches professional networks—partially. LinkedIn generates less interaction than Facebook, but you can use it to reach your professional networks with either brief updates or long blog-style posts. People check it less frequently than they check Facebook or Twitter. For anyone who's been in business a few years, it's a great way to build a list of connections and make an impression on them. As with Facebook and Twitter, don't expect 100% reach to your LinkedIn connections; most of them will miss what you posted.

Tumblr is awesome for reaching the young. If you remember 10cc and Peter Gabriel, you're too old for Tumblr. It's full of teens and millennials. Tumblr's design and audience make viral content spread rapidly. If you've got something cool to show or say, do it here. You can get people interested by tagging content with popular tags or reaching out to people with lots of followers.

Instagram, Pinterest, and Snapchat spread pictures better than they spread words. Make friends with a graphics person, and you can exploit these social networks. But since they're not about writing, they're beyond the scope of this book.

Message Without Messing Up

Short person-to-person messages are everywhere, not just on your phone's texting app. WhatsApp and WeChat go around the phone carriers. Google and Apple have messaging systems. Within corporations, people message on Slack, Microsoft Yammer, and salesforce.com's Chatter. Facebook, Twitter, LinkedIn, and Tumblr all have person-to-person messaging.

All these messages add to the continuous babble of our personal communication. While they don't demand an instant response like a phone call, they're more immediate than email. Used right, they get you just the result you're looking for in a hurry. Used wrong, they prove you're an annoying boor.

The overarching piece of advice on messaging systems is to

tread carefully and leave as light a footprint as possible. With
that philosophy, here are a few practical tips:

- **Reconsider messaging at all.** If you can get your task done
  without texting or sending an instant message, you're better
  off—it minimizes the chance to create annoyance.
- **Message down or across but generally not up.** Messages
  work best between friends and colleagues, within or outside
  a company. But messaging bosses is dicey, especially if they
  manage lots of potential texters. That said, your boss would
  probably appreciate a timely text in an emergency, like "The
  website is down and we're losing orders."
- **Avoid group texts.** Sometimes text messages can help a
  tightly knit group of two to four people communicate. I've
  used it with my coauthors to share our triumphs and photos
  on the road. But inviting a bunch of random people to a
  group text session multiplies the chance of annoyance geo-
  metrically.
- **Request an answer.** If you don't know what you want, don't
  message. If you've got an extended question, use email or
  a phone call. Messaging is for quick, urgent questions like
  "Where is the right logo graphic file?" or "Who is in charge
  of customer service now that Margot has left?" If the recipient can't respond in a quick message, don't use messaging.
- **Choose the right medium.** Texts and similar phone-based
  messages are good for people you know pretty well, those
  who would welcome a note from you. Corporate messaging
  systems function well for work-related questions that need
  a quick answer. Social network messaging is appropriate

between people who know and follow each other on these networks—Facebook friends, Twitter mutual followers, and LinkedIn connections.

- **Get right to the point.** Don't be coy. Practice extreme front-loading with a spoonful of politeness. For example, "If you have a minute, I could really use some help with a contact at Chrysler." Or "Wally, do you want me to check with Maribel before we make the customer data public this afternoon?" Don't ask, "Do you have a minute?" because the answer is typically no. If you feel the need to write two or three sentences, send an email instead.

- **Use links and photos where they make sense.** As in "Did you see our review in the *Times* [link]?" Or "Here's what the new mock-up now looks like [photo]."

- **Avoid text-speak and emojis.** In business settings, text-speak (cu l8r lol) saves a few characters at the expense of mystifying workers who didn't grow up texting. And unless you want to be perceived as an adolescent, the crying-face emoji isn't an appropriate way to note that you just pissed off a client.

- **Get off as quick as you got on.** Once you get your answer, the correct response is "Thanks," "Thx," or "Grateful, I will buy you a bottle of scotch the next time you are in town." Not "By the way, how did Billy's hernia surgery turn out?"

Make Cold Contacts with Social Network Messaging

In the previous chapter, I described the best email strategy to get people to help you. But what if you don't have their email addresses?

Every social network has a direct messaging channel. They're your secret weapons. Just don't wear out your welcome.

LinkedIn allows you to contact your professional connections, even if you've lost their professional email. That's especially helpful when people change jobs. (If you pay for LinkedIn Premium, you can also use LinkedIn to contact people you're not connected with.) The LinkedIn message also shows up in the recipient's actual email inbox, and they can reply from there or within LinkedIn. Once you've made contact, continue the back-and-forth through actual email.

Facebook's Messenger also allows you to send messages, although the ones to people you're not friends with end up in a separate, deprecated folder. And Twitter lets you send direct messages to those who follow you.

My experience with these channels, as both a sender and a recipient, is that people respond quickly to simple messages and with annoyance to longer, more elaborate requests. So tell someone very quickly who you are, explain what you want, and invite further contact. Here's an example you might send on LinkedIn or Facebook:

> Hi, Mr. Simon. I'm a fellow business-book author, and I've enjoyed your latest book "Message Not Received." I'd like to interview you for my blog. Are you open to it?

Corporate Social Networks

Workers must now deal with a (relatively) new phenomenon: social networks managed by companies. Tools such as Slack, HipChat, Microsoft Yammer, and salesforce.com's Chatter pull conversations out of email and put them where everybody, or at least everybody in the company who's interested, can look at them. And as I write this, Facebook is also announcing a corporate version of its social network.

So you can now get all the benefits—and potential embarrassment—of a social network within your company.

These tools include both person-to-person messaging and spaces where people can post. But don't think of them as time-wasting social networks. Think of them as productivity tools. And apply the corporate version of the Iron Imperative: Don't waste your coworkers' time.

Here are a few guidelines for this rapidly developing communications channel:

- **Be positive and professional.** These tools are like sending email, except that everyone can see most of the posts. Wasting time, using profanity, and expressing political sentiments are out of place. You're there to get work done and to help others do the same.
- **Keep requests and answers short.** Participants in these spaces typically are looking for help with something— solving a problem, working with a client, or hiring, for example. If you're going to post a question, take a moment and search the company's intranet (and the corporate social network) to make sure the answer isn't there already. Then pose your question in a few sentences. Long posts in these spaces waste even more of people's time than long rambling emails. If you see a question you can answer—or want to raise an issue with the question—then respond in a few sentences.

- Share files for longer information. These systems allow you to post content such as documents, presentations, and graphics. Post and link to these rather than typing hundreds of words of text directly in a post.
- **Start new groups and spaces only if you can maintain them.** Create a discussion space for your new project, and invite the whole team. If you've taken charge of the internal "quit smoking" group, by all means invite people to join and create a space for discussion. But these corporate social networks tend to have a lot of derelict spaces that people have started and abandoned. Don't start something unless you intend to run it.

23
Promote Intelligently

Imagine a communications channel that routinely bombards thousands of people with information that they don't care about. Imagine also that it delivers—in an old-fashioned, ritualized format—tiny particles of information surrounded with enormous helpings of jargon and other bullshit that completely overwhelm any speck of value. And imagine as well that every decent-sized company has people dedicated to the production of this drivel or hires expensive outside experts to create it on the company's behalf.

What I've just described, of course, is the modern machinery dedicated to the creation and distribution of press releases.

As an analyst, I was in the press-release target zone. I received several every day. Of the 10,000 press releases that landed in my inbox over the 20 years I worked as an analyst, only about 200 had even the tiniest amount of relevance. Even the ones that hit the target were 80% fluff. Do the math: that's 20,000 meaningful words out of a total production of 8.5 million, generating an infinitesimal 0.2% meaning ratio. A format that is 99.8% waste is a failure.

This failure operates at epic volume. The public relations industry distributes over a million press releases per year. That's half a billion wasted words in the vain hope of creating a little coverage. Somebody had to write those words. If that's you, I'm here to help you.

I am *not* declaring war on public relations. I have worked closely with some incredible PR people, both those who worked with me to promote my products and content and those who strove to influence me as an analyst. They are bright, humble, and unrelentingly helpful. I'm not here to destroy PR. I'm here to save it from its wasteful habit of writing and distributing meaningless fluff.

Promotion is a worthwhile activity—you have to tell people what your company is doing and why it's good. But press releases and other marketing-focused content, such as marketing web pages, are out of touch with the readers they're trying to reach and with the way we consume content now. I will explain how you can make your press releases and marketing pages bullshit-free. Given the geyser of bullshit that characterizes most marketing and PR writing, if you follow these tips, you'll certainly stand out.

Dissecting a Typical Press Release

Let's look at one of these beasts. I chose this one, not because it is particularly bad but because it is typical. In April 2015, hybris, a technology company that is part of the German software giant SAP, sent this 1,087-word release out to thousands of journalists, analysts, and other "influencers." I've deleted some of the most boring parts to save space.

hybris Monetizes Digital Transformation with Innovative Billing Solution

As Part of SAP® Solutions for Customer Engagement and Commerce, SAP® hybris® Billing Solution Allows Companies to Expand Their Product Offerings and Introduce Customer-Centric, Value-Based Services

April 30, 2015 08:00 AM Eastern Daylight Time

MUNICH—(BUSINESS WIRE)—hybris software, an SAP company, today highlighted the SAP® hybris® Billing solution as a core component of SAP® solutions for customer engagement and commerce to enable organizations to monetize digital transformation in today's highly competitive and fast-moving economy. [*About 200 words of jargon-laden techno-speak mercifully removed here.*]

"The digital transformation era has opened new doors for customers as well as companies. Now, customers have greater options for purchasing products and engaging with brands while companies enjoy a closer relationship with their customers, a constant cash flow and the ability to realize a greater lifetime value for each customer over time," said Brian Walker, chief strategy officer, Customer Engagement and Commerce, hybris and SAP. "The integration of SAP hybris Billing with the customer engagement and commerce platform fosters this relationship, eliminating the need for a separate platform to service these new revenue models while also providing the speed and efficiency needed to be successful." [*About 100 more words of drivel removed.*]

With companies now tasked with providing great customer service and highly technological, connected products on top of finding a new way of delivering, packaging, pricing and billing its value proposition to its customers, they are turning to SAP hybris Billing to:

• Bring innovative pricing offers to market faster than the competition with an intuitive user interface that requires zero coding.
• Support prepaid, postpaid and hybrid models to monitor customer accounts in real time and improve customer sentiment by giving subscribers control over their spending. [*Nearly 200 words in three more similar bullets, plus more quotes from executives removed.*]

To learn more about SAP hybris Billing, visit www.hybris.com/en/billing.

About hybris

hybris software, an SAP company, provides omni-channel customer engagement and commerce solutions that allow organizations to build up a contextual understanding of their customers in real time, deliver a more impactful, relevant customer experience and sell more goods, services and digital content across every touch point, channel and device. Through its state-of-the-art customer data management, context-driven marketing tools and unified commerce processes, hybris has helped some of the world's leading organizations, including

3M, ASICS. [*Another 94 words of boilerplate removed.*] For more information, visit www.hybris.com.

Any statements contained in this document that are not historical facts are forward-looking statements as defined in the U.S. Private Securities Litigation Reform Act of 1995. Words such as "anticipate," "believe," "estimate," "expect," "forecast," "intend," "may," "plan," "project," "predict," "should" and "will" and similar expressions as they relate to SAP are intended to identify such forward-looking statements. SAP undertakes no obligation to publicly update or revise any forward-looking statements. All forward-looking statements are subject to various risks and uncertainties that could cause actual results to differ materially from expectations. The factors that could affect SAP's future financial results are discussed more fully in SAP's filings with the U.S. Securities and Exchange Commission ("SEC"), including SAP's most recent Annual Report on Form 20-F filed with the SEC. Readers are cautioned not to place undue reliance on these forward-looking statements, which speak only as of their dates.

I computed the meaning ratio of this release, including the parts that I haven't reprinted here. Out of 1,087 words, 253 have meaning, for a sad little meaning ratio of 23%. Regrettably, this is typical of press releases.

Note the unconvincing time wasters:

- **The parade of super-duper superlatives.** Starting with its "innovative" solution, SAP and hybris bombard us with "sophisticated" multiparty settlements, "radically changed" customer experiences, "superlative" customer care, and "state-of-the-art" customer data management. Each superlative sets the reader's bullshit detector off. Taken together, they completely torpedo the credibility of the release.
- **The generic, meaningless quote.** I've actually worked with Brian Walker at a past job, and he never once said anything to me like "The integration of SAP hybris Billing with the customer engagement and commerce platform fosters this relationship, eliminating the need for a separate platform to service these new revenue models while also providing the speed and efficiency needed to be successful." These quotes mean nothing, neither here nor in an industry trade magazine if, by some fluke, they end up quoted.
- **The syrup of industry jargon poured over everything.** The release is attempting to communicate to journalists and businesspeople, in code, that the company is fully swaddled in the latest trends. That's why we need references to "digital transformation," shifting business models "disruptively," and "omni-channel customer engagement." Pulling these buzzwords from a bin and slathering them over the release

creates an uneven reading experience that flushes away any actual meaning.

- **The obligatory boilerplate disclaimer that undermines the whole release.** Nobody reads the financial bit about "forward-looking statements." But that disclaimer basically says, "You can't hold us to any of the promises you just read."

Rethinking Press Releases

Press releases started as a way to get coverage in newspapers and magazines. But now every reporter gets, and ignores, dozens of them every week. A typical release goes to at least 1,000 people. If you're lucky, two of those people respond and 998 of them just press Delete because they've gotten used to worthless releases.

This needs to change. And I'm not the only one who thinks so. Richard Edelman, CEO of Edelman, one of the top marketing and communications agencies in the world, told me, "Our clients are increasingly not asking for outbound shouting—they want new ways to connect with consumers." His company puts more effort into promoting the positions and brands of its clients through earned media—conversations that the company's own customers promote—and owned media (like blogs). Companies can publish content on sites like Medium and the *Huffington Post*. Influencing journalists is no longer the central element of the campaign, and press releases are no longer the best way to influence journalists.

Rick Clancy published or supervised thousands of releases during his tenure as head of public relations for the US electronics business of Sony Corporation. He's now a PR professor at the

University of North Carolina's School of Media and Journalism. He agrees that the era of "spray and pray"—of sending out releases broadly and hoping somebody will pick up on them—is over. But Clancy says that in a big company like Sony, the release serves a secondary function—focusing the company's internal perspective on product launch, acquisition, or executive hire. "If you have done it well, a press release is something that has been critically reviewed. It has been blessed that the information is accurate and is going to be out there and around for a while." Even so, Clancy occasionally needed to fight off the march of unsupported superlatives. "I did write 'Yuck!' on some drafts from my team and sent them back," he says. I respect Clancy's opinion and experience but have to wonder if there is a better way.

At the Coca-Cola Company, Ashley Brown, who headed digital communications for the company, told Ragan Communications, "I'm on a mission . . . what I want to do is kill the press release." The company has replaced many of its press releases with posts on its "Coca-Cola Journey" site, which features graphics, videos, and articles about the company's activities.

So along with Coca-Cola, Rick Clancy, and Edelman, let's rethink the press release.

The ROAM Analysis of a Press Release

What is a press release doing now? Here's a ROAM analysis:

- **Readers: anyone who can spread the word.** The target is no longer just journalists and analysts; it's anyone from mommy bloggers to nontraditional content sources like Upworthy and BuzzFeed—basically, anyone who can spread a story.

- **Objective: positive sentiment.** Get readers to believe the product is worthwhile and the company is good.
- **Action: spread the word.** Generating news stories used to be the ideal action. That's still useful, but now the release can get people to share information on social media as well.
- **iMpression: the PR person is valuable.** In the past as a PR person, you didn't care—you annoyed 998 people to get to the two who mattered. Now you're creating a relationship. Everything you send should say, "I know you, and I'm here to help you with information."

The Bullshit-Free Release

When you remove the jargon, the fluffy quotes, and the superlatives, what are you left with?

Facts.

Now let's add something back in: the direct voice of the company. Not in a stilted quote—in a sentence written directly from the spokesperson to the reader.

What you end up with is, basically, a blog post that says, "We did this, and here's why."

For example in 2015, Google executed a financial and organizational transaction. Here's what Google CEO Larry Page wrote to explain it.

Google Announces Plans for New Operating Structure
August 10, 2015

G is for Google.

As Sergey and I wrote in the original founders' letter 11 years ago, "Google is not a conventional company. We do not intend to become one." As part of that, we also said that you could expect us to make "smaller bets in areas that might seem very speculative or even strange when compared to our current businesses." From the start, we've always strived to do more, and to do important and meaningful things with the resources we have.

We did a lot of things that seemed crazy at the time. Many of those crazy things now have over a billion users, like Google Maps, YouTube, Chrome, and Android. And we haven't stopped there. We are still trying to do things other people think are crazy but we are super excited about.

We've long believed that over time companies tend to get comfortable doing the same thing, just making incremental changes. But in the technology industry, where revolutionary ideas drive the next big growth areas, you need to be a bit uncomfortable to stay relevant.

Our company is operating well today, but we think we can make it cleaner and more accountable. So we are creating a new company, called Alphabet. I am really excited to be running Alphabet as CEO with help from my capable partner, Sergey, as President.

What is Alphabet? Alphabet is mostly a collection of companies. The largest of which, of course, is Google. This newer Google is a bit slimmed down, with the companies that are pretty far afield of our main internet products contained in Alphabet instead. What do we mean by far afield? Good examples are our health efforts: Life Sciences (that works on the glucose-sensing contact lens), and Calico (focused on longevity). Fundamentally, we believe this allows us more management scale, as we can run things independently that aren't very related.

Alphabet is about businesses prospering through strong leaders and independence. In general, our model is to have a strong CEO who runs each business, with Sergey and me in service to them as needed. We will rigorously handle capital allocation and work to make sure each business is executing well. We'll also make sure we have a great CEO for each business, and we'll determine their compensation. In addition, with this new structure we plan to implement segment reporting for our Q4 results, where Google financials will be provided separately than those for the rest of Alphabet businesses as a whole.

This new structure will allow us to keep tremendous focus on the extraordinary opportunities we have inside of Google. A key part of this is Sundar Pichai. Sundar has been saying the things I would have said (and sometimes better!) for quite some time now, and I've been tremendously enjoying our work together. He has really stepped up since October of last year, when he took on product and engineering responsibility for our internet businesses. Sergey and I have been super excited about his progress and dedication to the company. And it is clear to us and our board that it is time for Sundar to be CEO of Google. I feel very fortunate to have someone as talented as he is to run the slightly slimmed down Google and this frees up time for me to continue to scale our aspirations. I have been spending quite a bit of time with Sundar, helping him and the company in any way I can, and I will of course continue to do that. Google itself is also making all sorts of new products, and I know Sundar will always be focused on innovation—continuing to stretch boundaries. I know he deeply cares that we can continue to make big strides on our core mission to organize the world's information. Recent launches like Google Photos and Google Now using machine learning are amazing progress. Google also has some services that are run with their own identity, like YouTube. Susan is doing a great job as CEO, running a strong brand and driving incredible growth. [*This is followed by 299 words about financials and strategy, which I've deleted.*]

Larry Page

CEO, Alphabet

There are still superlatives here, but now there are fewer of them because they're in the voice of the CEO, who doesn't want to sound stilted. There's a merciful lack of jargon. All the facts are still there, but you get a sense of what the CEO is aiming at. This was published as a blog post but also distributed as a press release. And it certainly generated plenty of coverage.

It's not just Google that's doing this. For example, Tesla Motors published a release titled "Tesla Model S Achieves Best Safety Rating of Any Car Ever Tested: Sets New NHTSA Vehicle Safety Score Record" in August 2013. The release explained why the new Tesla was more crash-proof than any other car, with actual physics and analogies ("Just like jumping into a pool of water from a tall height, it is better to have the pool be deep and not contain rocks."). There was no quote from Tesla executives, just facts.

You can do this, too. Here's how:

- **Write directly, in the voice of the spokesperson.** It could be the CEO, CMO, or head of PR.

- **Put the news in the title.** We are releasing a new product. We are acquiring a company. We are promoting someone.
- **Explain what you did and why it is important.** We launched a new product because our customers had a problem and we solved it. We acquired a company because it filled a hole in our offerings. We promoted someone because they are well suited to be the new CMO.
- **Use as many facts as possible.** Cite growth numbers, user numbers, new capabilities—and list them out factually.
- **Write it in an easily accessible fashion to maximize spread.** A release written like this stands out just because it is different. Write it in a conversational voice. More people will understand it. And if they do, more of them will share it.

If you can't fit your release into this format, maybe you shouldn't go to the trouble of sending it. If people who understood this sent fewer releases, there would be a lot less waste, and the inboxes of analysts and journalists would be a lot cleaner.

If you *do* write a release like this, you can spread it through the usual PR distribution channels. But you can also post it for your company's friends on Facebook and Twitter. If those friends read it and understand it, they will actually share it. And you'll get the attention you deserve.

For Other Marketing Pages, Write as Little as Possible

Let's talk about your company's website. I'm going to assume you don't work for a media company.

There are pages on it where your visitors can complete transactions—buy something, ask questions, or whatever action your customers need to take. Those pages earn their keep.

Maybe you have support pages, where people can look up answers to questions about your products. Those are useful.

There are pages where you post the stories you want to share. Those are blog pages. And if you've followed my advice, perhaps your press pages look like that, too.

Finally, there are the pages where you describe your company and your products. There's a good chance you'll have to write copy for pages like this. Over 60% of the writers in the WOBS Writing Survey wrote copy for the web.

I've read a lot of these pages. They're dreadfully bad. A committee decides how the company describes its mission, which results in a muddy, equivocal result. (Remember Ray's Helicopter from chapter 15?) The pages that describe products and companies tend to include lots of words. That's not going to work when people are reading on screens.

Remember, people who find these pages are asking the question, "Should I work with these guys?" If they give up on your text, you've lost them.

Company and product pages should be short. They should include bullets and graphics. They should be written with "we" to describe who you are, and "you" to include the customer.

If you have a long list of specs, link to it. Don't force us to wade through it.

Remember who's reading this stuff. Treat the reader's time as more valuable than your own.

24
Craft Actionable Reports

I wrote reports for a living for many years. One day, while I was giving my three-year-old a bath, he asked me what I did for work. How could I explain business strategy reports to a three-year-old? "I write stories about what is going to happen in the future," I told him. "And my stories help people in companies to make good decisions."

Three-year-olds love stories. So he responded, "Tell me one of your stories, Daddy." I told him this story, about how digital video recorders would transform television (this was in 1999, when TiVo was new):

Once upon a time there were some people who made television programs. Lots of people watched the television programs. And they also watched the commercials. This made the people who made the commercials happy, so they gave money to the people who made the programs. Those people used the money to make really good programs, so everyone was happy.

One day, some very smart people invented a magical machine. With the magical machine, you could watch the television programs any time you wanted, not just at the time that they were on. And you didn't need to watch the commercials.

The people who watched television thought this machine was wonderful, so they rushed out and bought those magical machines for themselves. Then they watched TV any time they wanted, and they didn't watch the commercials.

Unfortunately, this made the people who made the commercials very unhappy. "If no one watches our commercials," they said, "then we can't pay to put them on anymore." So they stopped paying the people who made the TV programs.

This made the people who made the TV programs very unhappy. "We need the money to make good television programs," they said. And since they didn't have enough money, they made bad programs instead of good ones.

Now there were only bad programs on TV. The people who watched TV were very unhappy because their magical machines couldn't find them any good programs to watch. The people who made the commercials were unhappy because no one would watch their commercials. And the people who made the programs were unhappy because they had no money to make good programs.

So they all lived unhappily ever after.

My report on digital video recorders used different words, but that was the story inside it. The businesspeople who read the report benefited from my research and statistics, but they *remembered* what I wrote because of the story, a story simple enough for a three-year-old to understand.

If you're writing a report, what's your story?

The ROAM Analysis of a Report

If you're working on a big writing project, there's a good chance it's a report of some kind. In the WOBS Writing Survey, 53% of business writers wrote reports for use inside their company, while 41% wrote reports for customers.

These reports vary greatly. Marketers write to impress customers, research people explain what their research has found, and managers analyze corporate data and decisions. But they're all longish pieces (at least 2,500 words) that set out to explain what is really happening, so readers can make better decisions.

Despite the variation in reports, the ROAM analysis of a report is pretty consistent:

- **Readers: decision makers interested in a topic.** Report audiences may be outside a company or within it, but either way, they need information to make a decision.
- **Objective: make people smarter.** Your goal is to make readers understand what you have learned.
- **Action: make informed decisions.** The report is successful if those who read it incorporate it into their decision-making. They either read the report and do something differently or use it to support a decision they were going to make anyway.
- **iMpression: the author is worth supporting.** Reports can save your job. When you do them well, readers say, "Ah, this is a good source of information for me." Some reports cost money; others, like white papers, generate marketing interest; others benefit internal audiences. But they all take effort

and cost money. If you make them valuable, you generate enough support to keep getting paid to do them.

The ROAM analysis also explains why all reports are stories. Readers understand stories. They remember them and share them with others. They find them valuable and support them. Even if two reports have equally valuable analysis, the one that is written as a story will be more effective.

The story aspect of reports explains their structure. They start with a descriptive title (and optionally, explanatory subtitle) and an executive summary that recaps the story. The story proper begins with a setup that describes the problem and continues with an analysis of what the various actors are doing and what's really happening in a market, or in a company. At the end, you get a satisfying set of recommendations. Anyone who works in Hollywood can relate to these pieces: setup, complications, and resolution. (Unlike Hollywood stories, the stories in reports are always supposed to be true.)

For your report stories to resonate, you need to build them from the right pieces, as the rest of this chapter explains (see figure 15).

Titles and Subtitles Should Be Both Catchy and Descriptive

There is no more important element to a report than the title. But you'd never know it from the report titles that are prevalent out there. Do you want to read "Human Development Report 2015"? What's in that report? You'd have to guess.

FIGURE 15. Parts of a report.

	How it advances the story	How to make it great	Ask yourself this	Tips
Title and subtitle	Gets reader interested	Be memorable, descriptive, and short.	How will it look in a search result?	Improve at the end of each draft.
Executive summary	Recaps the story in brief	Include vivid details from report.	Would this get me to read the report?	Write from scratch at the end of each draft.
Setup	Creates tension	Be clear about the problem to solve.	Have I asked a question worth answering?	Clearly cue up the next section.
Analysis	Resolves tension with knowledge	Use data to back up insights.	Have I made my case?	Use heads, bullets, and graphics.
Recommendations	Creates satisfactory conclusion	Be unequivocal.	Have I told the reader what to do?	Search and destroy weasel words.
End matter	Backs up analysis and conclusions	Be fastidious; source everything.	Would this convince doubters?	Include web links and methodology.

Compare that to some of these report titles:

How to Build Better Software, Faster

Five Ways Cloud Can Transform Your Business

Media Piracy in Emerging Economies

An ideal report title is memorable, descriptive, and short. Unfortunately, these goals contradict one another. Here's how to create a report title that works:

First, take a stab at the title at the start of each draft—and rethink it again at the end. Often the process of writing a draft kicks loose ideas and words that would make a great title.

Second, consider how the title will look in a web search. Effective titles include words that people search for, like "piracy" and "software." But even more important is how the title looks on a list of search results. Would you understand it in that context? Would you know what it represented? Would *you* click on it? Titles look different taken out of the context of the full report, but people searching don't see the context; they just see the title.

Third, don't forget the power of subtitles. Subtitles allow you to explain what the report is really about in eight or ten words. For example, "The Global Tech Market Outlook For 2016 To 2017: The Five Themes That Will Define Tech Spending In The Next Two Years." The subtitle (the part after the colon) does the descriptive work, allowing for a simpler title.

Executive Summaries Are Report Stories in Brief

Here's how most people write an executive summary: Wait until you finish the report. Then, before you need to turn it in, write a short description. Read each section, then summarize that section in a sentence.

That process generates a bland, homogeneous summary. That's unfortunate, because executive summaries are crucial.

People in a hurry read *only* the summary. The rest will decide to read the whole report based on what they read in the summary. A lame summary is deadly.

If the report is a story, the right executive summary is the same story, written briefly. It's intriguing if it includes the tidbits that make the report memorable: examples, statistics, metaphors. Imagine one of your readers sitting on a barstool next to you. They say, "What's the coolest stuff in this report? What did you find out?" Your answer, written directly to the reader, is the executive summary.

Don't wait until the end of the process to write the summary. Include a summary with every draft. Write the summary at the end of the draft, when the ideas are fresh in your mind. At the end of the next draft, write it again—from scratch. If your summary is a paragraph or two (shorter is better), then these rewrites won't take up much time. But the act of writing a summary for each draft—and improving it with comments from your editor—will create a summary that sings. And that will do your report justice.

The Setup and Analysis Must Create Tension, Then Resolve It

In the body of the report, you tell the story. You set up the problem, reveal what you found in your research, make observations, explain the consequences of those observations, and take the analysis as far as you can.

Apply the lessons of chapters 3 through 10 of this book: Eliminate passive voice, jargon, and weasel words; write directly to the reader with "we" and "you"; and deploy numbers and examples throughout the text.

Well-researched reports can be very detailed and chewy. To make them useful, make them skimmable. Here's where you take the lesson of chapter 11 to heart: *paragraphs suck*. Prose is hard to parse. In its place, use these elements:

- **Short sections with descriptive section heads** make scanning easy, with no more than two levels of heading.
- **Bullets with bold openers** (like this one) make the main points easy to identify.
- **Numbered lists** are more effective than bullets when the list has a natural sequence, like a set of steps.
- **Tables** can replace bulleted or numbered lists when the items have a parallel structure.
- **Graphics**, such as charts and conceptual graphics, break up the text and communicate concepts alongside them.
- **Case studies** make report stories come alive.
- **Sidebars** allow you to pull out interesting material that's not central to the story.

A reader scanning a report written with these elements can perceive the story by scanning the heads and bold bullet openers, reviewing the graphics, or reading the prose beginning to end. The more ways you have of communicating the story, the greater the chance that the reader will retain it.

Conclusions and Recommendations
Justify the Report's Value

Why am I bothering to read your report?

Because I intend to make a decision based on what I am reading.

A report that doesn't include conclusions and recommendations is incomplete. As Forrester's James McQuivey, who has written countless great reports, explains, "Many writers fall short of compelling content because they refuse to follow an idea to its logical conclusion." You have wasted the reader's time, in violation of the Iron Imperative.

At the end of your analysis, tie everything together; then tell the reader what to do.

This is where the weasel words creep in because telling people what to do—and generalizing to all your readers—seems fraught with danger. Do not yield. Readers seeking guidance will be grateful for your recommendation. Those with a strong perspective of their own will be pleased that you made a clear argument for your recommendations, even if they disagree with them.

End Matter Proves You Did Your Homework

Some stuff is just too tedious to include in the text of a report. It interrupts the story. For example, no one wants to wade through footnotes, extended digressions, data methodologies, or bibliographic details as they're reading.

Put this stuff at the end, in its own section. This enables the curious to go deeper into what you wrote about, while making it easy for the rest of the readers to skip it.

Some Report Process Tips

A report is a big job. Process makes all the difference, not only in how it comes out but also in how you feel while you're doing it. To be effective, rather than frustrated, here is where to apply the process advice in chapters 12 through 19 and the tips in chapters 5 and 11:

- Spend half of the process on research and the other half on writing and revising (see chapters 12 and 14).
- Do a ROAM analysis to be clear with all your collaborators, editors, and reviewers about what you're aiming at (see chapter 13).
- Work with an editor who stands in for the reader and advises you what's working and what's not (see chapter 15).
- Use research plans and fat outlines to communicate with editors and collaborators, even before you reach the drafting stage (see chapter 14).
- Manage your reviewers for effective collaboration (see chapter 17).
- Develop graphics in parallel with the text (see chapter 11).
- Write titles and summaries at each stage (see chapter 5).

In my years as a researcher and report writer, these process tips saved me from anguish and enabled me to create some pretty good reports.

EPILOGUE
Change the Bullshit Culture

You've changed yourself. You now write without bullshit. You stand out in your workplace.

It's time to give back.

If you've changed yourself, how can you change your company, your department, or your workgroup?

Your job is to spread the Iron Imperative:

Treat the reader's time as more valuable than your own.

Your organization will make great strides if clarity becomes a core value. Then you can all spend your time being productive instead of parsing blather-laden emails and documents. Organizational change is a big job, but it's worth it.

Start by recruiting powerful friends. Clear writing gets you noticed. Pay close attention to who's noticing you. It could be your boss, an HR person, the manager in the next cube with 12 years' seniority, or the senior vice president who shared some kind words with you at the quarterly department lunch. Ask them to support your effort to change the culture of communication; then bring them a plan.

Focus your effort. People who attempt to change everything end up changing nothing. Limit your scope; pick your battles.

Focus on mass emails, training classes, or PowerPoint presentations. Root out jargon, limit word counts, or improve graphics. Choose a team or department where you have managerial support. For example, you might propose to reduce jargon in all emails that people in the product management group send to at least five other people. It's easier to succeed this way than to quixotically take on the whole culture at once.

Then prove your worth. Gather some statistics: "Our work group produces 200 reports per year, and 20% of clients say that they are too long"; or "Office workers spend 14% of their time on email." Then show how your proposal will help. People want to believe that it's worthwhile to clear the bullshit, but if you're spending time on it, your bosses will expect proof that the time will not be wasted.

Your plan should include measurable results. How will you spread the word—meetings, emails, training, social media, intranet? Will you recruit volunteers into an army of irregulars? What stages will your program go through? How will you measure results? Unless you've got clear goals that managers and collaborators can get behind, your effort is just a hobby and unlikely to succeed.

Don't go it alone. Your friends and colleagues aren't just pawns in your scheme. They're teammates. Listen to, build on, and amplify their good ideas.

Learn what not to change. If your senior management just rolled out a new strategy, it's probably filled with buzzwords like "Six Sigma" or "customer experience." Those are not the jargon words to take on. If your senior vice president bloviates like a politician, perhaps her emails are not the ones to single out for opprobrium. As the Serenity Prayer says, you must acquire the serenity to accept the things you cannot change, the courage to change the things you can, and the wisdom to know the difference. Bullshit fighters who lack that wisdom become roadkill.

Build on your successes. It took six months, but you purged most of the jargon from your reports. Have a glass of champagne, then take on passive voice, or confusing graphics, or weasel words. Or move beyond reports to emails and blog posts, or beyond your department to the whole division. There's always more bullshit to fight. Only wimps rest on their laurels.

Email me to tell me how you are doing. My email address is josh@bernoff.com. I would like nothing better than to hear about your successes.

And visit my site at withoutbullshit.com. Share the tools and graphics and ideas that you find there. Spread the word as broadly as you can.

Together we can help the world to understand the value of writing without bullshit. And then, perhaps, we'll all be able to get a little more work done.

Acknowledgments

Writing this book has been the most rewarding professional experience of my life. For decades, I've longed to share what I've learned about writing and telling the truth. Now you hold it in your hands.

I would have had nothing to say if it were not for the mentors who taught me to write well. Thanks to M. C. Speece, Dena Brody, Jon Waldron, Jack McGrath, Mary Modahl, and Bill Bluestein.

Twenty years at Forrester Research made me the writer that I am today. I am deeply (watch those qualifiers!) indebted to George F. Colony, who created the culture on whose anvil I was forged. My key collaborators at Forrester included Emily Nagle Green, Chris Charron, Charlene Li, Ted Schadler, Harley Manning, Kerry Bodine, James McQuivey, Julie Ask, Michael Gazala, David Cooperstein, Cliff Condon, and many, many other smart people. This book could not possibly exist without the knowledge and skills they taught me.

I tapped a band of irregulars to refine everything I wrote. These generous people included Jeremiah Owyang, Nate Elliott, Shar VanBoskirk, Rick Clancy, Brian McNely, Miguel Fernandez, Glenn Engler, Gale Stafford, Dustin Moody, Ted Schadler (again), David Moldawer, Rohit Bhargava, Lionel Menchaca Jr., Len Burman, and Louis Biggie. Thanks also to my promotional and spiritual advisors, Ad'M DiBiaso, Jens Kueter, Phil LeClare, Laura Moran, and Chris Syme.

Merlina McGovern is my favorite copy editor, and she keeps me from making too many stupid writing mistakes. She deserves extra chocolate. Jim Spencer created my home base for this book, withoutbullshit.com.

I'm grateful for the active and intelligent community that supports and challenges me daily on Facebook, on Twitter, and on my blog. You are my silent collaborators.

This book came into being through the hard work of my agents, Katherine Flynn and Ike Williams, and my editors at HarperBusiness, Stephanie Hitchcock and Hollis Heimbouch.

Finally, and above all, thanks to my family: Kimberley, Ray, and Isaac; and Mom, Dad, Andy, Tom, Marj, and Curt. You always believed in me. That made all the difference.

Notes

Chapter 1: Transcend Bullshit

7 **On its website, under "Who We Are," is this description:** "Who We Are" page at Inovalon.com, retrieved February 15, 2016. See http://wobs.co/WWBinovalon.

14 **"This will only get worse":** "Ten Heretical Thoughts About Advertising" by Tom Cunniff, on the blog *Cunniff*, September 25, 2014. See http://wobs.co/WWBcunniff.

15 **"We are all writers":** From *Everybody Writes: Your Go-To Guide to Creating Ridiculously Good Content* by Ann Handley (Wiley, 2014), front flap. See http://wobs.co/WWBhandley.

Chapter 2: Seize Your Opportunity

18 **"strangling in unnecessary words, circular constructions, pompous frills, and meaningless jargon":** From *On Writing Well* by William Zinsser (Harper & Row, 1985), p. 7.

18 **"one of the most salient features of our culture is that there is so much bullshit":** From *On Bullshit* by Harry G. Frankfurt (Princeton University Press, 2005), p. 1.

18 **I conducted the WOBS Writing Survey from January through March 2016:** For the WOBS Writing Survey, I recruited survey respondents from several sources. I emailed readers of my blog and people who signed up for a webinar on clear writing. I also recruited respondents through posts and advertisements on my blog, Twitter, LinkedIn, and Facebook. To be included in the sample set, respondents needed to answer all substantive questions, say that they write for two or more hours per week at work (excluding email), and write primarily in English. Of the 793 people who responded, 547 fit these criteria. Where I cite a

statistic that says that a specific percentage of respondents believe a statement, that statistic indicates the number who checked the top two boxes on a five-point Likert scale from "completely disagree" to "completely agree." Because of the way in which I recruited these respondents, they do not represent a random sample of American business professionals—the sample is biased toward people who are more concerned about the quality of writing at work. If this were a random sample, then statistics based on a sample this size would have a margin of error of plus or minus 5% (at a 95% confidence level).

19 **According to Forrester Research, among adults who are online, seven out of ten already use smartphones:** From "The State of Consumers and Technology: Benchmark 2015, US" by Gina Fleming, *Forrester Report,* September 28, 2015, p. 2. Available to Forrester Research Technographics clients at http://wobs.co/WWBforrester.

19 **91% are reading email, and 75% are doing social networking:** From "2014 Mobile Behavior Report," Salesforce Marketing Cloud, p. 13. Available at http://wobs.co/WWBsalesforce.

20 **"Babies born today will probably never read anything in print":** Quoted from "'Is Print Dead?' and Other Tough Topics from the MPA Conference" by Emma Bazilian, *Adweek,* October 16, 2012. See http://wobs.co/WWBhorowitz.

20 **it was easiest to concentrate when reading material in print compared to on a screen:** For more detail, see the book *Words Onscreen: The Fate of Reading in a Digital World* by Naomi S. Baron (Oxford University Press, 2015). More about Naomi Baron at http://wobs.co/WWBbaron.

26 **"its tendency to stunt students' critical thinking abilities":** From "The Ill Effects of the Five Paragraph Theme" by Kimberly Wesley, *English Journal* (September 2000): pp. 57–60. See http://wobs.co/WWBwesley.

26 **86% admitted that they used complicated language in papers to sound more sophisticated:** "Consequences of Erudite Vernacular Utilized Irrespective of Necessity: Problems with Using Long Words Needlessly" by Daniel M. Oppenheimer, *Applied*

Cognitive Psychology 20 (2006): pp. 139–56. See http://wobs
.co/WWBoppenheimer.

Chapter 3: Move Beyond Fear
38 **But instead, he wrote this:** "Flaming Notebook" by Lionel
Menchaca, on the blog *Direct2Dell*, July 13, 2006. See http://
wobs.co/WWBmenchaca.
39 **ultimately agreeing to replace over 4 million batteries:** "Dell
to Recall 4 Million Batteries" by Tom Krazit, *CNET News*, December 20, 2006. See http://wobs.co/WWBdell.
39 **he wrote this at the top of the editorial page:** "We Apologize
to Our Loyal Readers" by John W. Henry, *Boston Globe*, January 5, 2016. See http://wobs.co/WWBhenry.
40 **Deborah Tannen explores these perceptions in her book**
Talking from 9 to 5: From *Talking from 9 to 5* by Deborah
Tannen (William Morrow, 2001), p. 42.

Chapter 4: Write Short
43 **"During revision, I realize that 90 percent of my cuts are
helpful":** From *How to Write Short: Word Craft for Fast Times*
by Roy Peter Clark (Little, Brown, 2013), p. 12. See http://wobs
.co/WWBclark.
48 **intended to explain the changes at the division, to all Nokia
employees:** "Stephen Elop's Email to Employees," from Microsoft's
website, posted July 17, 2014. See http://wobs.co/WWBelop.
50 **a world record for burying the lede:** Journalists say "bury the
lede." Other people say "bury the lead." I'll go with the former,
but if you prefer the latter, just pretend I wrote it that way.

Chapter 5: Front-Load Your Writing
55 **"give the summarizing idea before you give the individual
ideas being summarized":** *The Pyramid Principle: Logic in Writing and Thinking* by Barbara Minto (Prentice Hall, 2009), p. 9.
See http://wobs.co/WWBminto.
58 **was simply called "Innovation":** "The Full *New York Times*
Innovation Report" by Jason Abbruzzese, *Mashable*, May 16,
2014. See http://wobs.co/WWBnytimes.

Chapter 6: Purge Passive Voice

61 **"Attention must be paid by zombies":** I didn't invent the zombies test. See, for example, this tweet by Marine Corps University ethics professor Rebecca Johnson from October 18, 2012: http://wobs.co/WWBjohnson.

63 **with the passive constructions highlighted in bold:** "Assessing the Olympics: Preliminary Economic Analysis of a Boston 2024 Games Impacts, Opportunities and Risks" by the UMass Donahue Institute for Economic and Public Policy Research, March 2014. See http://wobs.co/WWBolympics.

65 **"Clayton Christensen in his pioneering book *The Innovator's Dilemma*":** From *The Future of the Internet and How to Stop It* by Jonathan Zittrain (Yale University Press, 2008), p. 83. See http://wobs.co/WWBzittrain.

66 **"A white paper is considered to be a standard marketing tool today":** "Effective Business Writing: The White Paper" by Anjana Srikanth, *Internet Writing Journal*, September 2002. See http://wobs.co/WWBsrikanth.

66 **"is increasingly provided through community and home-based services":** "Connecting Health and Care for the Nation: A Shared Nationwide Interoperability Roadmap," Executive Summary, by Office of the National Coordinator for Health Information Technology, February 2015. See http://wobs.co/WWBhealthcare.

Chapter 7: Replace Jargon

68 **a new version of a "business intelligence" product:** "Oracle Business Intelligence 12c Helps Organizations Boost Their Digital Transformation Through Agile Visual Analytics," press release in Newsroom at Oracle.com, November 12, 2015. See http://wobs.co/WWBoracle.

70 **Steven Pinker describes the "Curse of Knowledge":** From *The Sense of Style: The Thinking Person's Guide to Writing in the 21st Century* by Steven Pinker (Viking, 2014), p. 57. See http://wobs.co/WWBpinker.

71 **"If you can't explain it simply, you don't understand it well**

enough": For more insights from Phil Simon, refer to *Message Not Received: Why Business Communication Is Broken and How to Fix It* (Wiley, 2015). See http://wobs.co/WWBsimon.

71 **Here's one from a healthcare consultant**: "Thought Leadership" page on Bluespoon Consulting site, retrieved December 25, 2015. See http://wobs.co/WWBbluespoon. (Website is no longer live.)

72 **Compare it to this mission statement from Google**: "About Google" page on Google site, retrieved February 15, 2016. See http://wobs.co/WWBgoogle.

72 **Original (from an email about healthcare information strategies for America)**: "CODA: The Back Story, Part 4" by Hunt Blair, *Collaborate or Fail: Building the Digital Infrastructure of the Learning Health System*, June 14, 2015. See http://wobs.co/WWBcollaboration.

Chapter 8: Eliminate Weasel Words
77 **which he wrote to show how VMware can help corporate chief information officers:** "CIOs Redefining Role to Fuel Integration, Innovation" by Pat Gelsinger, March 5, 2015. See http://wobs.co/WWBgelsinger.

78 **"As soon as you add an intensifier, you're turning an all-or-none dichotomy into a graduated scale":** From *The Sense of Style: The Thinking Person's Guide to Writing in the 21st Century* by Stephen Pinker (Viking, 2014), p. 45. See http://wobs.co/WWBpinker.

80 **it took me 15 seconds to look it up:** From "Corporate Fact Sheet" on the United news page, retrieved February 15, 2016. See http://wobs.co/WWBunited.

80 **Bernie Sanders's website, regarding the Black Lives Matter movement:** From "Issues: Racial Justice" on the Bernie 2016 website, retrieved February 15, 2016. See http://wobs.co/WWBsanders.

81 **Here's a typical sentence from Pakes's response:** Matt Pakes's response to "Theft, Lies, and Facebook Video" by Hank Green, medium.com, August 3, 2015. See http://wobs.co/WWBpakes.

Chapter 9: Be Direct

88 **company overview from the Avaya corporate website:** "Company Overview" page from the Avaya website, retrieved February 15, 2016. See http://wobs.co/WWBavaya.

90 **but take a look at how simply Google describes its number one priority:** "Ten Things We Know to Be True" page from the Google website, retrieved February 15, 2016. http://wobs.co/WWBphilosophy.

Chapter 10: Use Numbers Wisely

92 **who really wants to prevent the sexual exploitation of children:** I'm indebted to Carl Bialik for this example. It's from the article "Retirement Is Long Overdue for Some Aging Statistics" by Carl Bialik, *Wall Street Journal*, April 22, 2005. See http://wobs.co/WWBbialik.

92 **in the *Australian* newspaper, she wrote:** "Filters Needed to Battle Child Porn" by Bernadette McMenamin, *Australian*, January 8, 2008. See http://wobs.co/WWBmcmenamin.

95 **"1 million IoT devices will be purchased and installed every single hour":** "Top Strategic Predictions for 2016 and Beyond: The Future Is a Digital Thing" by Daryl C. Plummer et al., *Gartner Report*, October 2, 2015. Accessible to Gartner account holders at http://wobs.co/WWBgartner.

95 **"TV has declined roughly 4%":** "Online Video Streaming Up 60%, TV Consumption Down but Not Out [Report]" by Andy Smith, *ReelSEO: The Video Marketer's Guide*, December 9, 2014. See http://wobs.co/WWBreel.

96 **about its new software VestVision:** "HD Vest and Wealthcare Capital Extend Collaboration with Launch of Next Generation Goals-Based Investing and Financial Planning Software," press release on *Market Wired*, December 3, 2015. See http://wobs.co/WWBvest.

96 **British people spend an average of £800 a year on Christmas presents:** "Average British Family to Spend £800 on Christmas" by Press Association, *Telegraph*, December 8, 2015. See http://wobs.co/WWBtelegraph.

97 **The correlation coefficient is about 99%:** From *Spurious Cor-*

relations by Tyler Vigen (Hachette, 2015), pp. 48–49. See http://wobs.co/WWBvigen.

97 **income has grown nearly six times more under Democratic presidents:** "Want a Better Economy? History Says Vote Democrat!" by Adam Hartung, *Forbes*, October 10, 2012. See http://wobs.co/WWBhartung.

98 **"George W. Bush could not get out before the financial crisis":** "Timing Is Everything," *Economist*, August 9, 2014. See http://wobs.co/WWBeconomist.

100 **"satisfied and confident in the government's performance,"** **according to the Associated Press:** "Thai Junta Says 99 Percent of People Are Happy with Its Rule" by Nattasuda Anusonadisai, *Yahoo! News*, December 23, 2015. See http://wobs.co/WWBthai.

100 **2.0% is less than 2.1% and greater than 1.9%:** "U.S. Economy Grew at 2 Percent Rate over Summer; A Pickup Is Seen" by Martin Crutsinger, *San Jose Mercury News*, December 22, 2015. See http://wobs.co/WWBeconomy.

102 **any Republican candidate in a head-to-head battle:** "Poll: Hillary Clinton Losing to Everybody" by Mike Flynn, *Breitbart*, November 23, 2015. See http://wobs.co/WWBbreitbart.

102 **Donald Trump would beat Hillary Clinton, 46% to 41%:** "Fox News Poll: 2016 Matchups; Syrian Refugees," *Fox News*, November 20, 2015. See http://wobs.co/WWBfoxnews.

102 **according to a Quinnipiac poll of 1,453 registered voters:** "Latest Poll: Sanders Handily Trounces All Top Republicans— Yeah, Including Trump" by Janet Allon, *Alternet*, December 2, 2015. See http://wobs.co/WWBalternet.

103 **"rather than to seek out evidence that might disprove it":** "How to Ignore the Yes-Man in Your Head" by Jason Zweig, *Wall Street Journal*, November 19, 2016. See http://wobs.co/WWBconfirmation.

103 **"only reads to their children an average of 25 hours":** "Celebrate Reading" by Angela Marino, United Way of Greater Saint Louis website, March 2, 2011. See http://wobs.co/WWBreads.

104 **this number is a great example of statistics abuse:** "It Seems

to Exist, But How to Measure Class Gap in Reading?" by Carl
Bialik, *Wall Street Journal,* June 15, 2007. See http://wobs.co/
WWBabuse.

105 **"eclipsing the middle class's share":** "Charting Trump's Rise
Through the Decline of the Middle Class" by Dan Balz, *Washington Post,* December 12, 2015. See http://wobs.co/WWBtrump.

Chapter 11: Reveal Structure

109 **marketers' misguided use of social media:** "Burn It Down,
Start from Scratch and Build a Social Media Strategy That
Works" by Augie Ray, *Experience: The Blog,* August 21, 2015. See
http://wobs.co/WWBray.

111 **eye-catching graphic (see figure 6):** "Societal: The Third Di-
mension of Modern Day Brand Building" by David Armano,
Logic + Emotion, October 26, 2014. See http://wobs.co/
WWBarmano.

112 **to become a better writer, I came up with a simple chart (see
figure 7):** "The Only Way to Become a Better Writer" by Josh
Bernoff, *Without Bullshit,* June 1, 2015. See http://wobs.co/
WWBpractice.

113 **Edward Tufte's *The Visual Display of Quantitative Information*:** *The Visual Display of Quantitative Information* by Edward
Tufte (Graphics Press, 2001). See http://wobs.co/WWBtufte.

114 **people shared the table graphic across the web thousands of
times (see figure 8):** "10 Top Writing Tips and the Psychology
Behind Them" by Josh Bernoff, *Without Bullshit,* May 4, 2015.
See http://wobs.co/WWBwriting.

116 **enhance the meaning and make the page more interesting:**
For instructions on how to embed a tweet, see http://wobs
.co/WWBtweet. For instructions on how to embed a YouTube
video, see http://wobs.co/WWByoutube.

Chapter 13: Think First

132 **"12 Handy Tips for Running Better Remote Meetings":** "12
Handy Tips for Running Better Remote Meetings" by Lindsay
Kolowich, *HubSpot Blogs,* December 22, 2015. See http://wobs
.co/WWBhubspot.

Chapter 14: Plan Purposefully

136 **(which was the actual title of a report I wrote)**: "How To Create a Social Application For Life Sciences Without Getting Fired" by Josh Bernoff, *Forrester Report,* April 20, 2009. Available to Forrester Research clients at http://wobs.co/WWBsocial.

Chapter 16: Find Flow

150 **Kurt Vonnegut Jr. published the short story "Harrison Bergeron"**: "Harrison Bergeron" by Kurt Vonnegut Jr. Full text available at http://wobs.co/WWBharrison.

152 **"you forget yourself and your surroundings"**: From *Writing in Flow: Keys to Enhanced Creativity* by Susan K. Perry (Writer's Digest Books, 1999), p. 1.

155 **"An electric circuit seemed to close; and a spark flashed forth"**: "Letters describing the Discovery of Quaternions" by William Rowan Hamilton, August 5, 1865, retrieved from the History of Mathematics web pages of Trinity College, Dublin, on February 15, 2016. See http://wobs.co/WWBhamilton.

Chapter 21: Email Thoughtfully

194 **She calls it "email apnea"**: "Are You Breathing? Do You Have Email Apnea?" by Linda Stone, *Linda Stone* (blog), November 24, 2014. See http://wobs.co/WWBstone.

194 **the average businessperson sends or receives 121 emails per day**: "Email Statistics Report, 2014–2018," by Sara Radicati, Radicati Group, April 2014. See http://wobs.co/WWBradicati.

196 **come back to bite you if one of the recipients reveals what you were trying to hide**: The only acceptable use for Bcc is to email a bunch of people at once without revealing their email addresses to one another—sort of a poor man's mailing list server.

198 **with the decline starting at a length of 100 words**: "7 Tips for Getting More Responses to Your Emails (with Data!)" by Alex Moore, *Boomerang,* February 12, 2016. See http://wobs.co/WWBboomerang.

199 **including reporters, to help deliver the paper**: "Here's the Union Letter Asking *Globe* Staffers to Deliver the Paper" by

Dan Kennedy, *Media Nation,* January 2, 2016. See http://wobs
.co/WWBglobe.

202 **a high of 29% (for emails about hobbies) to a low of 14% (for
    emails about daily deals):** "Average Email Campaign Stats
    of MailChimp Customers by Industry," on the MailChimp
    website, accessed February 15, 2016. See http://wobs.co/
    WWBmailchimp.

204 **"speaking to me in the first person (use *I* or *we* and *you*) with
    natural-sounding language":** From *Everybody Writes: Your
    Go-To Guide to Creating Ridiculously Good Content* by Ann Han-
    dley (Wiley, 2014), p. 221. See http://wobs.co/WWBhandley.

206 **he needed to cut 8% of his staff:** Email: "A More Focused
    Twitter" by Jack Dorsey, October 13, 2015, posted on the US
    Securities and Exchange Commission website, accessed Feb-
    ruary 15, 2016. http://wobs.co/WWBdorsey.

Chapter 22: Master Social Media
214 **yearns to be a lion tamer:** "Vocational Guidance Counsellor"
    sketch by Monty Python. Script at http://wobs.co/
    WWBpython.

216 **career paths for corporate social media strategists got viewed
    over 30,000 times (see figure 14):** "Altimeter Report: The Two
    Career Paths of the Corporate Social Strategist. Be Proactive
    or Become 'Social Media Help Desk'" by Jeremiah Owyang,
    Web Strategist, November 10, 2010. See http://wobs.co/
    WWBaltimeter.

220 **Guy Kawasaki and Peg Fitzpatrick's *The Art of Social Media*:**
    Refer to *The Art of Social Media: Power Tips for Power Users* by
    Guy Kawasaki and Peg Fitzpatrick (Portfolio, 2014). See http://
    wobs.co/WWBsocialtips.

Chapter 23: Promote Intelligently
228 **over a million press releases per year:** This is a very rough esti-
    mate but is most likely low. See "How Many Press Releases Are
    Sent Out Each Day" by Jeremy Porter, *Journalistics,* March 22,
    2009. See http://wobs.co/WWBreleases.

229 **thousands of journalists, analysts, and other "influencers":**

"hybris Monetizes Digital Transformation with Innovative Billing Solution," SAP press release on Business Wire, April 30, 2015. See http://wobs.co/WWBhybris.

235 **"what I want to do is kill the press release":** "Coca-Cola Digital Chief: 'Kill the Press Release'" by Russell Working, ragan.com, December 23, 2013. See http://wobs.co/WWBcoke.

236 **Here's what Google CEO Larry Page wrote to explain it:** "G Is for Google" by Larry Page, *Google Official Blog,* August 10, 2015. See http://wobs.co/WWBabcxyz.

239 **"Sets New NHTSA Vehicle Safety Score Record" in August 2013:** "Tesla Model S Achieves Best Safety Rating of Any Car Ever Tested," press release on Tesla Motors website, August 19, 2013. See http://wobs.co/WWBtesla.

Chapter 24: Craft Actionable Reports

245 **Do you want to read "Human Development Report 2015":** "Human Development Report 2015" by United Nations Development Programme (UNDP) (Selim Jahan, lead author), 2015. See http://wobs.co/WWBhuman.

247 **"The Five Themes That Will Define Tech Spending In The Next Two Years":** "The Global Tech Market Outlook For 2016 To 2017" by Andrew Bartels, *Forrester Report,* January 5, 2016. Available to Forrester Research clients at http://wobs.co/WWBthemes.

Bibliography

Baron, Naomi S. *Words Onscreen: The Fate of Reading in a Digital World*. New York: Oxford University Press, 2015.

Beard, Henry, and Christopher Cerf. *Spinglish: The Definitive Dictionary of Deliberately Deceptive Language*. New York: Blue Rider Press, 2015.

Beckwith, Lois. *The Dictionary of Corporate Bullshit: An A to Z Lexicon of Empty, Enraging, and Just Plain Stupid Office Talk*. New York: Broadway Books, 2006.

Clark, Roy Peter. *How to Write Short: Word Craft for Fast Times*. New York: Little, Brown, 2013.

Csikszentmihalyi, Mihaly. *Flow: The Psychology of Optimal Experience*. New York: HarperPerennial, 1991.

Elbow, Peter. *Writing with Power: Techniques for Mastering the Writing Process*. 2nd ed. New York: Oxford University Press, 1998.

Frankfurt, Harry G. *On Bullshit*. Princeton, NJ: Princeton University Press, 2005.

Fugere, Brian, Chelsea Hardaway, and Jon Warshawsky. *Why Business People Speak Like Idiots: A Bullfighter's Guide*. New York: Free Press, 2005.

Handley, Ann. *Everybody Writes: Your Go-To Guide for Ridiculously Good Content*. Hoboken, NJ: Wiley, 2014.

Huff, Darrell. *How to Lie with Statistics*. New York: Norton, 1954.

Lamott, Anne. *Bird by Bird: Some Instructions on Writing and Life*. New York: Anchor Books, 1995.

Li, Charlene, and Josh Bernoff. *Groundswell: Winning in a World Transformed by Social Technologies*. Boston: Harvard Business Review Press, 2008.

Minto, Barbara. *The Pyramid Principle: Logic in Writing and Thinking.* 3rd ed. Harlow, UK: Financial Times Prentice Hall, 2009.

Norris, Mary. *Between You & Me: Confessions of a Comma Queen.* New York: Norton, 2015.

Perry, Susan K. *Writing in Flow: Keys to Enhanced Creativity.* Cincinnati: Writer's Digest Books, 1999.

Peters, Mark. *Bullshit: A Lexicon.* New York: Three Rivers Press, 2015.

Pinker, Steven. *The Sense of Style: The Thinking Person's Guide to Writing in the 21st Century.* New York: Viking, 2014.

Reinhart, Alex. *Statistics Done Wrong: The Woefully Complete Guide.* San Francisco: No Starch Press, 2015.

Roman, Kenneth, and Joel Raphaelson. *Writing That Works: How to Communicate Effectively in Business.* 3rd ed. New York: Harper-Collins, 2000.

Shipley, David, and Will Schwalbe. *Send: Why People Email So Badly and How to Do It Better.* New York: Vintage Books, 2010.

Simon, Phil. *Message Not Received: Why Business Communication Is Broken and How to Fix It.* Hoboken, NJ: Wiley, 2015.

Strunk, William, Jr., and E. B. White. *The Elements of Style.* 4th ed. New York: Longman, 2000.

Tannen, Deborah. *Talking from 9 to 5: Women and Men at Work.* New York: William Morrow, 1994.

Thomas, Francis-Noël, and Mark Turner. *Clear and Simple as the Truth: Writing Classic Prose.* 2nd ed. Princeton, NJ: Princeton University Press, 2011.

Vigen, Tyler. *Spurious Correlations.* New York: Hachette, 2015.

Webb, Nick. *The Dictionary of Bullshit: A Shamelessly Opinionated Guide to All That Is Absurd, Misleading and Insincere.* Naperville, IL: Sourcebooks, 2006.

Zinsser, William. *On Writing Well: An Informal Guide to Writing Nonfiction.* 3rd ed. New York: Harper & Row, 1985.

Index

action, in ROAM analysis, 130
active voice, rewriting in, 66–67
adjectives. *See* weasel words
Adobe Illustrator, 113
adverbs. *See* weasel words
advertising, 14
Alphabet, 236–39
Alternet, 102
Armano, David, 111–12
Art of Social Media, The, 220
attention spans, 19–21
audience. *See* readers
Australian newspaper, 92
Avaya, 88–89

Baron, Naomi S., 20
Bcc, 196
Be Paranoid Early, 123–24
Bialik, Carl, 93, 104
bias, 102–3
blog posts, 213–18
   about writing, 213–14
   front-loading, 59–60
   graphics in, 216, 217
   promoting on social networks,
      217
   reasons to blog, 213
   ROAM analysis of, 133, 214–15
   target sentence for, 215

titles, 59, 216
where to blog, 215
WordPress platform, 216
Boston Globe, 39, 199–200
Breitbart, 102
brevity, 43–54
   editing for, 184
   in corporate social networks, 226
   in messaging systems, 224
   tips for, 53
Brown, Ashley, 235
bullets, 46, 109–11
   in reports, 249
bullshit
   causes of, 18–28
   changing bullshit culture,
      253–54
   defined, 7
   history of, 18
   jargon, 68–75
   measuring, 7
   passive voice, 61–67
   pervasiveness of, 3
   weasel words, 76–83
   writing without. *See* writing
      without bullshit
burying the lede, 50, 184
   in managers' emails, 205
buzzwords. *See* jargon

C Space, 11–13
career
  clear writing as opportunity,
    28–29
  fear interferes with, 33
  how writing helps, 10–15
case studies, 249
causality
  economic, 97–98
  justifying, 97–100
Chartbeat, 20
Chatter, 222, 225
child pornography, 92–93
chunking content, 109–11
Clancy, Rick, 234–35, 257
Clark, Roy Peter, 43
Clinton, Hillary, 102
coauthors, 165–67
Coca-Cola, 235
collaboration, 157–67
  tools for, 162–65
  using Microsoft Word or
    Google Docs, 164
  with multiple authors, 165–67
Colony, George F., 257
commands, 85
Communispace. See C Space
concentration, attaining, 152–54
confirmation bias, 102–3
containers, 191–93
  list of, 193
content marketing, 15
  defined, 132
  ROAM analysis of, 132–34
context, 94–97
Cook, Scott, 146
copy editing, 178
copy editors, 161–62
correlation, 97

creativity, 144–49
  generating ideas, 147–49
  importance of deadlines to, 148
  strategies for, 146–47
criticism, 168–80, See also reviews
  criticism sandwich, 183
Csikszentmihalyi, Mihaly, 151
Cunniff, Tom, 13–14, 45
Curse of Knowledge, 70

data. See numbers
deadlines
  drive creativity, 148
  include in email, 198
Dell, 14, 38–39
  Michael Dell, 39
Delli-Colli, Kevin, 93
digital video recorders, 242, 243
documents
  executive summary, 58–59
  front-loading, 58–59
  reports, 242–51
Dorsey, Jack, 206–8
Dow Jones Industrial Average,
    94–95
Draft stage, 124–25
Dropbox, 163

economy
  income inequality, 105
  US, 97–98
Edelman (agency), 111, 201, 234
Edelman, Richard, 201, 234
editing, 181–87
  decline of, 21–25
  for brevity, 184
  for jargon, 185
  for passive voice, 184
  for weasel words, 185

numbers, 186
self-editing, 45
structural, 186
writing shorter, 43–54
editors, 158–59, 163
choosing, 176–78
copy editors, 161–62
types of, 176–78
working with, 175–80
edits. *See* reviews
Einstein, Albert, 71
Elop, Stephen, 47–54
email, 194–211
and smartphones, 209
cold emails, 200–202
connotations of, 191
elements of, 197–99
email apnea, 194
etiquette for, 208–11
for marketing, 202–4
frequency, 204, 205
from managers, 47–54, 205–8
front-loading, 56–58
include deadlines in, 198
length of, 58, 203, 205
open rates, 202–3
purposeful approach, 195
recipient list, 196
Reply All problem, 210
ROAM analysis of, 196–97
signature, 199
subject line, 56–58, 197, 203
target sentence for, 197
time spent on, 194
to research targets, 139, 200
tone in, 208
emojis, 224
end matter, in reports, 250
Evernote, 138, 148, 165

Everybody Writes, 15
executive summaries, 58–59
of reports, 247–48
when to write, 126, 248

Facebook, 81
for research, 139
messaging on, 222, 225
posting on, 218, 221
fact checkers, 161–62
failure, recovering from, 154–56
fat outline, 140–43
collaborating on, 166
defined, 141
fear
causes weasel words, 82
moving beyond, 33–42
writing boldly when afraid,
38–40
filenames, 59, 164
first person, 86–87
Fitzpatrick, Peg, 220
five-paragraph essay, 26
flow, 150–56
defined, 151
Forbes, 23, 216
formats, 191–93, *See also*
containers
prevalence of, 193
Forrester Research, 19, 144–46,
147, 203, 257, 289
Forum Corporation, 10
Fox News, 102
Frankfurt, Harry G., 18
front-loading, 55–60, 126

Gartner, 95
Gelsinger, Pat, 77
gender. *See* women

Google, 90–91, 236–39
  Alphabet, 236–39
  Google Docs, 116, 164
  Google Drive, 163
  Google rankings, 59
  Google Sheets, 138, 164
  mission statement, 72
  press release from, 236–39
  use of we/you, 90–91
Grammarly, 65
graphics, 47, 111–14
  in blog posts, 216, 217
  in reports, 249
  tools to create, 113
Green, Hank, 81
Groundswell, 212, 289
growth rates, 97, 101

Hamilton, William Rowan,
  154–55
Handley, Ann, 15
Hanes, 204
Harrison Bergeron, 150–51
Hartung, Adam, 97
HD Vest, 96
headings, 109–11
Henry, John W., 39
Hessan, Diane, 10–13
HipChat, 225
Horowitz, Ben, 20
HubSpot, 132–34
Huffington Post, 23, 216, 234
Human Development Report
  2015, 245
hybris, 229–34

I, used in writing, 86–87
idea development, 147–49, 176
  editing for, 186

Illustrator, 113
impression, in ROAM analysis, 131
income inequality, 105
Inovalon, 7–10
insider bias, 70–71
Instagram, 222
Intuit, 146
Iron Imperative, 5–6
  defined, 5
  demands brevity, 43
  in marketing emails, 203
  requires revealing structure, 108
  spreading, 253

Jager Adams, Marilyn, 104
jargon, 68–75
  defining terms, 75
  editing for, 185
  in managers' mails, 205
  in press releases, 233
  insider bias causes, 70–71
  legally required, 75
  rewriting, 71–73
  when to use, 74–75
Johnson & Johnson, 73, 89–90

Kassar, Barak, 129
Kawasaki, Guy, 220
Kolowich, Lindsey, 132
Kraft Foods, 204

lede. *See* burying the lede
legal requirements, 75, 160
Li, Charlene, 212, 257
Lilienfeld, Scott, 103
line editing, 177
LinkedIn
  blogging on, 215
  for research, 139

messaging on, 222, 225
posting on, 218, 221
links, 116
lists, 109–11
in reports, 249

MailChimp, 202–3
mailing lists, 196
managers
email from, 47–54, 205–8
role in document review,
160–61
tone in writing, 85
marketing
content marketing, 15, 132–34
email for, 202–4
marketing communications,
192, 228–41
press releases, 192, 228–40
web page copy, 240–41
Matrix, The, 117
McMenamin, Bernadette, 92
McQuivey, James, 153, 179, 250,
257
Meaning Ratio, 6–10, 228, 233
defined, 9
Medium, 215, 234
Menchaca, Lionel, Jr., 14, 38–39
Message Not Received, 71
messaging, 222–24
brevity, 224
methodology, 103–5
sources, 104
Microsoft, 47–54
OneNote, 138
PowerPoint, 113
Word, 116, 164
Yammer, 222, 225
Minto, Barbara, 55

mission statements. See purpose
statements
Monty Python, 214
Munoz, Oscar, 79–80

Naslund, Amber, 41
National Center for Missing and
Exploited Children, 92
New York Times, 58
Nokia, 47–54
numbers, 92–106
bias, 102–3
correlation, 97
editing, 186
growth rates, 97, 101
importance of context, 94–97
in press releases, 240
justifying causality, 97–100
methodology behind, 103–5
precision, 100–102
sample size, 104
sources, 104

objective, in ROAM analysis, 130
Olympics, 63–64
open rates, 202–3
opening sentences, 135–37
Oracle, 68–69
outlines. See also fat outline
limitations of, 140
Owyang, Jeremiah, 216, 217, 257

Page, Larry, 236, 239
Pakes, Matt, 81
paragraphs, why they suck, 108,
249
passive voice, 61–67
becoming aware of, 64–65
causes of, 65–66

passive voice (*cont.*)
  defined, 61
  editing, 184
  rewriting, 66–67
  why problematic, 62–64
  zombies test, 61
Perry, Susan K., 151
Pew Research Center, 105
phones. *See* smartphones
Pichai, Sundar, 238
Pinker, Stephen, 70, 78
Pinterest, 222
PowerPoint, 113
PR. *See* public relations
practice, value of, 113
precision, 100–102
  significant digits, 101
Prepare stage, 123–24
press releases, 192, 228–40
  bullshit-free, 236–40
  ROAM analysis of, 235–36
  titles, 240
process, 121–27
  Draft stage, 124
  for coauthoring, 165
  for collaboration, 157
  for writing reports, 251
  Prepare stage, 123–24
  Revise stage, 125
  three stages, 123–27
procrastination, 121
project managers, 158–59
pronouns (I/we/you), 84–91
  rewriting with, 87–91
proofreading, 178
public relations, 14, 228–40
purpose statements, 7–10
  Avaya, 88
  Google, 72

Inovalon, 7–10
  on websites, 241
  Ray's Helicopter, 169–75
Pyramid Principle, The, 55

qualifiers, 76–83, *See also* weasel
  words
quaternions, 155
Quicken and Quickbooks, 146
Quinnipiac, 102
quotations, 116
  in press releases, 233

Ray, Augie, 109–10
Ray's Helicopter, 169–75
readers
  in ROAM analysis, 129–30
  value of readers' time, 5–6
  visualizing, 73–74, 84–86,
    129–30
reading
  harder on a screen, 19–21
  poor comprehension, 20
ReelSEO, 95
reports, 242–51
  avoiding paragraphs in, 249
  avoiding weasel words in, 250
  conclusions, 250
  connotations of, 192
  executive summaries, 247–48
  graphics in, 249
  making skimmable, 249
  parts of, 245–51
  process tips for, 251
  ROAM analysis of, 244–45
  stories in, 242–43, 242–43, 248
  subtitles, 247
  titles, 245–47
  types of, 244

research, 137–40
emails to research targets, 139, 200–202
researchers, 159
tracking in a spreadsheet, 138–39
reviewers, 159–60, 163, 176–78
copy editors, 161–62
gatekeepers, 160–61
types of, 176–78
reviews
addressing, 179–80
copy edits, 178
editing, 181–87
exposing your flaws, 178
line edits, 177
managing, 122, 125, 168–80
psychology of, 168–69, 175
structural edit, 177
Revise stage, 125
ROAM analysis, 128–34
defined, 128, 129
edits helped by, 176
in editing, 186
of blog post, 214–15
of content marketing, 132–34
of email, 196–97
of press release, 235–36
of report, 244–45
of social networks, 219
target sentence, 131
Royal Canadian Mounted Police (RCMP), 92–93

salesforce.com, 19
Chatter, 222, 225
sample size, 104
Sanders, Bernie, 80
SAP, 229–34

Schadler, Ted, 257
Schindler, Esther, 14–15, 55, 78
Schwartz, Josh, 20
second person (you), 84–86
sections, 109, 249
Sense of Style, The, 70, 78
SEO (search engine optimization), 59, 218
Serenity Prayer, 254
shit sandwich, 183
sidebars, 249
significant digits, 101
Simon, Phil, 71
skimmability, 107–16
Skype, 165
Slack, 222, 225
smartphones
don't compose email on, 209
reading on, 19
Snapchat, 222
social media, 109–10, 212–27, *See also* social networks
blogs, 213–18
connotations of, 192
social networks. *See also* social media
choosing among, 220–22
cold contacts on, 224–25
corporate, 225–27
Facebook, 221
LinkedIn, 221
messaging on, 222–24
posting frequency, 220
posting on, 218–22
promoting blog posts on, 217
ROAM analysis of, 219
target sentence for, 219
Tumblr, 222
Twitter, 221

Sony, 234–35
Spurious Correlations, 98
statistics. *See* numbers
Steeves, Scott, 199
stock market, 94–95
Stone, Linda, 194
stories, in reports, 242–43
structure, revealing, 107–16
    with editing, 186
    with graphics, 111–14
    with headings and lists, 109–11
    with quotes and links, 116
    with tables, 114–15
subject line, email, 56–58, 197
    for marketing emails, 203
subtitles, of reports, 247
summaries. *See* executive
    summaries
superlatives, 233

tables, 46, 114–15
    in reports, 249
Tannen, Deborah, 40
target sentence
    for blog post, 133, 215
    for coauthored documents, 166
    for content marketing, 133
    for email, 197
    for social networks, 219
    in ROAM analysis, 131
terminology. *See* jargon
Tesla Motors, 239
text messaging, 222–24
    group texts, 223
Thailand, 100
three *P*s process, 121
titles
    of blog posts, 216
    of press releases, 240

of reports, 245–47
    when to write, 126, 135–37
TiVo, 242
Tufte, Edward, 113
Tumblr, 222
Twitter, 206–8
    for research, 139
    messaging on, 222
    posting on, 218, 221

United Airlines, 79–80
United Way of Greater Saint
    Louis, 103, 104
University of Massachusetts, 63
US Bureau of Labor Statistics, 105
US Customs and Border
    Protection, 93

VanBoskirk, Shar, 203
Vigen, Tyler, 98
*Visual Display of Quantitative
    Information, The*, 113
VMware, 77
Vonnegut, Kurt, Jr., 150–51

Walker, Brian, 230, 233
Wall Street Journal, 77, 93
Washington *Post*, 105
we, used in writing, 87
weasel words, 47, 76–83
    defined, 76
    editing for, 185
    eliminating, 79–82
    examples of, 76–79
    in press releases, 233
    in reports, 250
    problems caused by, 76–79
    replacing, 82
web pages, writing for, 240–41

WeChat, 222
WhatsApp, 222
WOBS Writing Survey, 18, 21, 27,
    42, 46, 69, 86, 93, 175, 241,
    244
    flaws in writing, 43–44
    jargon in, 69
    passive voice prevalance, 64
    prevalence of writing formats,
       193
    social network postings, 218
    time spend on email, 194
    use of statistics, 93
women
    benefit from direct writing,
       86–87
    challenges in business culture,
       40–42
    impress through writing, 42
word count, 45
WordPress, 116, 216
writing
    blog post about, 213–14
    brevity, 43–54
    creating a writing space, 153
    drafting, 124–25
    email, 194–211

flow, 150–56
front-loading, 55–60
how fear impairs, 33–42
how to concentrate, 152–54
must create change in reader,
    128
planning for, 135–43
preparing for, 128–34
process, 121–27
promotional, 228–41
teaching of, 25–28, 108
top writing tips, 115
value of practice, 113
with a coauthor, 165–67
writing without bullshit
    boosts career, 10–15
    bullshit-free press release,
       236–40
    changing bullshit culture,
       253–54
    risks of, v

Yammer, 222, 225
you, used in writing, 84–86

Zinsser, William, 18
zombies test, 61, 63

About the Author

Authors generally write this page about themselves but in the third person, perpetuating the charade that someone else is writing about them. I think that's bullshit, so I've written my biography myself.

In 35 years as a writer, I've written just about everything but fiction—software documentation, online help files, press releases, newsletters, magazine articles, web copy, over a hundred research reports, and four books. My blog, withoutbullshit.com, generated one million page views in its first 12 months.

My first book, *Groundswell: Winning in a World Transformed by Social Technologies* (Harvard Business Review Press, 2008), written with Charlene Li, was a *BusinessWeek* best seller. Abbey Klaassen, the editor of *Advertising Age*, picked it as "the best book ever written on marketing and media." I also cowrote *Empowered: Unleash Your Employees, Energize Your Customers, Transform Your Business* (Harvard Business Review Press, 2010), with Ted Schadler, and *The Mobile Mind Shift: Engineer Your Business to Win in the Mobile Moment* (Groundswell Press, 2014), with Ted Schadler and Julie Ask.

For 20 years, I was a principal analyst and senior vice president of idea development at Forrester Research, the elite technology research company. In that position, I wrote reports, gave speeches all over the world, and worked with Fortune 500 clients on business strategy. At Forrester I invented Technographics, the segmentation on which the company's consumer survey business is based. I analyzed the publishing, television, and music industries. I predicted the impact of technologies like video streaming, social media, and mobile applications. I appeared on *60 Minutes* and got quoted everywhere from the *Wall Street Journal* to *TV Guide*. The Society for New Communications Research recognized me as "Visionary of the Year."

Before Forrester I worked for startup companies including Software Arts, the company that invented the spreadsheet. I also spent three years as a PhD candidate and National Science Foundation Fellow in mathematics at MIT. My bachelor's degree is from Penn State.

I live in the Boston area with my wife; as I write this, my two children are in college. I'm the CEO of a nonprofit, wellnesscampaign.org, dedicated to the pursuit of wellness through changing habits. I like recreational cycling and cracking wise in front of audiences.

If you want to follow what I'm doing now, subscribe to my blog, withoutbullshit.com, where I post every weekday about writing, fighting bullshit, politics, nutrition, and whatever else I'm working on. You can follow me on Facebook or on Twitter as @jbernoff. I look forward to hearing from you.